unchurching

Christianity Without Churchianity

Richard Jacobson

First Edition

Cover design, layout and illustrations by Richard Jacobson

ISBN: 978-0692749951

Published by Unchurching Books

To my wife Beth and our children,
Joseph, Ariel, and Joshua.
I owe you everything.

Table of Contents

Part Three: Church Incorporated

Part Four: Church Outside the Box

Acknowledgments

This book wouldn't even exist if it weren't for several friends and family members who generously invested their time, talents and continual words of encouragement. At the top of this list are my wife and children. They supported me during the long journey of working through these ideas, even before I realized I was writing a book. I honestly can't put their immense contribution into words. Beth, Joseph, Ariel, and Joshua, thank you again.

Sadly, my mom passed away unexpectedly, shortly after I gave her the nearly-finished draft of this book. As far as I know, she never got to read all of it. However, she didn't need to read it because we already lived so much of it. Though we only experienced seasons of genuine church community while I was growing up, they planted the seeds that eventually produced this book. For that reason above all else, I have to say thanks, mom.

My dear friend Brenda Noel was one of the first people to hear my crazy ideas about church and insisted I turn them into a book. I'm also indebted to her for editing the final draft. And I'm very grateful to Gunnar Falk, and Stephen and Kaley Mayer for taking on the unenviable task of reading my earlier drafts and suggesting numerous improvements. Similarly, I must thank Glendo Grider for challenging some of the half-formed ideas in the previous draft.

I'm truly honored Jon Zens volunteered his expertise to help straighten out some of the more scholarly sections and write such an excellent foreword. Thank you Felicity Dale, Jeremy Myers and Keith Giles for your incredible endorsements and support. Thank you again Ralph Polendo from Quoir Publishing for giving feedback about the book layout, cover, and more.

I'm sure any writer can attest to the fact that you need a quite, private, and very comfortable place if you intend to write for hours at a time. Many thanks to my mother-in-law Terri Schneider and my wife Beth for the hours of toil they invested in renovating my home office so I could have such a place.

Thank you Kathy Harris from the Divine Detour blog for legitimizing me with my very first interview about Unchurching. Likewise, thank you Thomas Fortson for turning me into a real "professional author" by buying the first copy, even while the final edits were still underway. And thank you Tony Mize for taking the initiative to line-up my first book signing.

I also need to say a big thank you to all the friends and followers of my blog. You've supported me since day one. And even as I write this, many of you are actively spreading the word about this book through social media, email, and word-of-mouth. It's incredibly humbling and I truly can't thank you enough. I hope this book encourages you, much like you have encouraged me.

Foreword by Jon Zens

In the past ten years, that which calls itself "church" has gone through monumental upheaval. Church buildings are closing left and right, churches are going bankrupt at an alarming rate and, as usual, churches are splitting every moment. But the really noticeable trend in this current disruption is the huge number of people who have been—for a number of reasons—leaving the institutional churches. The religious buzz is about the "dones" and the "gones." Traditionally in America there was among many citizens the deeply rooted practice of "going to church." But those days are over. Getting up on Sunday morning and packing the family into a car to go to a building no longer has the pull it once had.

Many nervous church leaders with obvious vested interests will respond to the exodus from their buildings by saying that people are losing interest in God. But the truth is, as Clyde Reid pointed out in 1966, "To reject the institutional churches is not the same as rejecting God or rejecting the Christian faith ... Some people may have to reject the churches to find Christ and vitality ... And God is surely present outside the churches—often more present without than within."

When people exit churches, some find alternatives, but many still haven't found what they're looking for. Richard Jacobson's *Unchurching* will go a long way to helping believers realize that community around Christ is the unchartered longing in so many hearts. Most religious structures do not encourage and foster relationships. M. Scott Peck noted in 1987 that "the plain reality is that by and large the Church has not been in the community game; it has been in the numbers game."

Those who have come to feel uneasy about what goes on in the mainline churches, and those who have actually left, are faced with many valid questions and concerns. *Unchurching* seeks to help readers wrestle with a host of assumptions concerning "church," in order that the core of what following Christ in community really is will become more evident.

Sad to say, the journey out of institutional churches usually involves scrapping the layers of human traditions we've absorbed, and starting over with Christ from scratch. Frederick Buechner observed that what goes on in AA groups, "Is far closer to what Christ meant his church to be, and what it originally was, than much of what goes on in most churches I know … They make you wonder if the best thing that could happen to many a church might not be to have its building burn down and to lose all its money. Then all that the people would have left would be God and each other."

Unchurching will help you capture a vision for a fresh start that is built upon the Lord Jesus Christ, the only foundation the Father has put His seal upon.

- Jon Zens, author of *A Church Building Every 1/2 Mile: What Makes American Christianity Tick?* and editor of *Searching Together* since 1978

Introduction

"In the beginning the church was a fellowship of men and women centering on the living Christ. Then the church moved to Greece, where it became a philosophy. Then it moved to Rome, where it became an institution. Next, it moved to Europe, where it became a culture. And, finally, it moved to America, where it became an enterprise."

~ Richard Halverson

A Crisis of Faith

In 2003, I quit my full-time job as a pastor because I was having a crisis of faith. I wasn't having doubts about God or even doubts about the church. I was having doubts about the way we were doing church. I began to see a huge disconnect between the early churches described in the Bible and today's churches. The first churches were simple Christian communities; legally speaking, most of today's churches are corporations.

My first church experiences were on the opposite end of the spectrum from the church corporation. My childhood took place during the Jesus Movement. Depending on how you look at it, the Jesus Movement was either a Christian movement that was an offshoot of 70's hippie culture or a hippie movement that was an offshoot of 70's Christian culture. Either way, it was a far cry from today's church culture.

My earliest memories of church life happened in living rooms, coffee shops, bookstores, restaurants and, for a brief time, a Christian commune. I wasn't even aware that most Christians dressed up on Sundays and piled into cars to drive to special buildings to worship God. Nor could I imagine church gatherings in which believers just sat, passively listening to sermons. For me, church life was completely different.

Whenever we gathered, believers brought Bibles, guitars and tambourines. We ate together, sang together, prayed and laughed with one another, and read passages of scripture to each other. Believers shared stories about the things God was saying and doing in their lives. People gave their lives to Christ, gave up addictions, and were miraculously healed at every turn. Miracles became so commonplace in our gatherings, they were simply expected.

It wasn't until I was almost a teenager that I first set foot in a church building. It was then that I encountered questions like, "What church do you go to?" Prior to that, I didn't even know church could be a separate thing I could "go to." As far as I knew, church was simply something you were, like a family; such questions made as much sense as asking, "What family do you go to?" But over time I learned to speak the same language and learned to do church just like everybody else.

Actually, I probably did church a little more-so than everybody else. By the time I was in my early twenties, I was singing on the worship team, teaching Sunday School, volunteering in the youth ministry, performing in church plays, and doing lots of free graphic design and video editing for my church. Plus, I used my vacation days from work to help with week-long church events like short-term mission trips and Vacation Bible School. Basically, I invested all my energy, talent, and time into my church. And I can honestly say I loved every minute of it.

Though it was a completely different form of church, God seemed every bit as present in the midst of all the pre-planned services and expensive programs as he had been during the impromptu gatherings in living rooms and coffee shops I had known as a kid. Since I already spent most of my time at church, I guess it was inevitable I would eventually end up on staff. Becoming a full-time pastor was wonderful. I was fortunate enough to work in a healthy church with very little dysfunction or politics. I was surrounded by people I really loved, doing work I really loved. It was my dream job.

But then God began leading me down a different path. Slowly, he began to reveal things through his Word that seemed to point toward a disconnect between the churches described in the Bible and the kind of church model we employ today. At first I tried to fight it.

I told myself the dilemma was all in my head; God wasn't really speaking to me. I sought counsel from fellow pastors and church elders, asking them to help me find biblical answers to my growing list of troubling questions. But every time they patiently walked me through the Scriptures, it would only lead to more questions.

For a long while, I feared I was becoming a heretic. Eventually, I had to trust it was the Lord's leading. So I quit pastoring, quit attending the institutional church, and started searching for a church community that looked more like the churches described in the Bible. My search was very long and very painful. Many friends seemed to think I was falling away from the faith instead of actively pursuing it.

The fact that I couldn't really articulate what was going on only made matters worse. Whenever I ran into a former fellow church member, they would ask why I no longer attended. But I could only provide half-formed, unsatisfactory explanations. Often, they would remind me, "There's no such thing as a perfect church." Sadly, I didn't know how to explain I wasn't looking for a perfect church; I was looking for an authentic one. Clearly, I needed to sort out my views on church and learn how to articulate them.

For a long time, I had been writing down all the things I thought the Lord was speaking to me about the church. Those personal study notes eventually grew into a huge pile, more than enough material for a single book. So I tried writing a book. But the task proved far too daunting at the time. However, I knew I needed to do something to get my thoughts in order and get them out into the world.

For years, I had made a living as a graphic designer and illustrator. Plus, I had always dabbled in animation. So I decided to start an animated video and cartoon blog about church. Because the blog was mostly for me, I half-jokingly titled it *Church Anarchist*. This was not only a nod to my seemingly anti-authoritarian church views, but it was a nice tribute to my 80's upbringing. (It seemed like every cool kid in the 80's imagined he was some kind of teenage anarchist.) It also sounded way cooler than *Church Egalitarian*. But because the name always required a bit more explanation than it was worth, it eventually became the *Unchurching* blog.

Most of my posts took the form of short, animated talks that tackled various aspects of today's institutional church. In order to limit the videos to about four minutes each, I could only touch on certain topics but by-and-large, they turned out pretty well. Almost immediately, I began receiving emails and comments from viewers who told me the videos really impacted them. Some said the videos helped them work up the courage to leave abusive church situations. Others gathered like-minded friends and began pursuing genuine church community together.

In just a matter of months, the videos started racking up thousands of views and getting noticed by several Christian authors. Some of these authors have become long-distance friends and I've been able to meet a few of them in person. The whole experience has been really exciting.

Even more exciting were the messages I received from pastors. In hindsight, I think I sold my fellow pastors short. I assumed they would all denounce me and my blog. Instead, I received several private messages from pastors who secretly agreed with the blog and wanted advice on what to do about it. For reasons that will hopefully become clear in the latter part of this book, I encouraged a lot of them to keep their positions in the institutional church. I think having an "anti-institutional-church guy" encourage them in their calling was just as shocking to them as their support was to me.

Best of all, the blog became the catalyst for me to find genuine church community again. Thanks to those animations and cartoons, I connected with people all around the world who were on a similar journey. As it turns out, a few of them were right here in my own back yard. A follower of the blog invited me to lunch and introduced me to a brother who connected me to a local community of believers. Currently, we are learning what it means to become a genuine church community, instead of a church corporation. Sharing life with this group has been great and it's part of what gave me the resolve to finally finish this book.

I don't think God spoke to me all those years about church just to motivate me personally. If the goal was to simply call me away from the institutional church, all my memories of non-institutional church life could have been enough to make me homesick and motivate me to leave. Instead, he chose to lead me through a long and arduous deconstruction of the institutional church model. I would like to believe this was so I could encourage other believers who are struggling with church-as-usual—those who have a nagging feeling that something just isn't right with today's church model, yet can't quite put their finger on the problem or how to articulate it.

If that's you, I hope the very existence of this book testifies to the fact that you are not alone. But even more than that, I hope it illuminates what the Bible really has to say about church, without distorting it through the lens of man-made tradition. I hope it gives you a glimpse God's true vision for his church. And I hope you realize his vision is so much more compelling than what you were previously taught. His vision is the spiritual community you were created for.

Part One: Spiritual Community

"The aim of God in history is the creation of an all-inclusive community of loving persons with God himself at the very heart of this community as its prime Sustainer and most glorious Inhabitant."

~ Dallas Willard

A Peculiar People

Before the birth of the church, believers had limited access to God. They had to go to a special place (known as a temple) and enlist the aid of a special person (known as a priest) in order to worship their God. And even then, they couldn't actually get close to him. The priest had to serve as a mediator between the people and their God. However, God had something better in mind. One day, everything would change, especially the way God's followers would relate to him. In Jeremiah 31:34 he promised:

> And no longer shall each one teach his neighbor and each his brother, saying, "Know the Lord," for they shall all know me, from the least of them to the greatest, declares the Lord.

Likewise, in Joel 2:28, 29, he said:

> And it shall come to pass afterward, that I will pour out my Spirit on all flesh; your sons and your daughters shall prophesy, your old men shall dream dreams, and your young men shall see visions. Even on the male and female servants in those days I will pour out my Spirit.

But exactly how did God plan to accomplish this? By sending his Son Jesus Christ to save us from the sin that separated us from our God. In Matthew 1:21–23 we are told:

> "She will bear a son, and you shall call his name Jesus, for he will save his people from their sins." All this

took place to fulfill what the Lord had spoken by the prophet: "Behold, the virgin shall conceive and bear a son, and they shall call his name Immanuel" (which means, God with us).

Whereas other people only imagined a god somewhere above us, Christians boasted of a God who left his heavenly realm to be right here with us. Whereas other religions required people to make sacrifices to their gods, Christians told the story of a God who sacrificed himself for his people. That sacrifice not only atoned for our sins, it opened the door for God to come and dwell in the midst of the spiritual community, known as the *church*.

The word church can apply to either the church universal or to a local church fellowship. The church universal includes all believers around the world, past, present and future. A local church fellowship is a small group of family, friends, and neighbors who comprise a Christian community, somewhat like an extended spiritual family. The single most defining characteristic of the early church was that God was clearly present in their communities.

Early Christianity was radically different from the religion of both the Jews and the Gentiles (meaning the non-Jews). Christianity probably didn't even look like a religion to many people; it seemed more like a movement. The people who were swept up in this movement didn't follow religious practices as much as live a particular lifestyle. This lifestyle not only went against the grain of secular culture, it was completely contradictory to many people's religious sensibilities at the time. It was even different from what many would recognize as Christianity today.

Instead of worshiping God in special, sacred buildings, church members worshiped God in their own ordinary homes.[1] Not only that, they went so far as to claim they themselves were the real temple of God.[2] And instead of employing special priests, they viewed every believer as a fellow priest.[3] Consequently, average church members were expected to carry out all the priestly duties in the church, such as confessing their sins to one another and praying for healing.[4]

---

1   **Romans 16:5** Greet also the church in their house.

    1 Corinthians 16:19 Aquila and Prisca, together with the church in their house, send you hearty greetings in the Lord.

    Colossians 4:15 Give my greetings to the brothers at Laodicea, and to Nympha and the church in her house.

    Philemon 2 And Apphia our sister and Archippus our fellow soldier, and the church in your house …

2   **1 Corinthians 3:16, 17** Do you not know that you are God's temple and that God's Spirit dwells in you? If anyone destroys God's temple, God will destroy him. For God's temple is holy, and you are that temple.

3   **1 Peter 2:9** But you are a chosen race, a royal priesthood …

4   **James 5:16** Therefore, confess your sins to one another and pray for one another, that you may be healed. The prayer of a righteous person has great power as it is working.

Rather than somber religious ceremonies, they frequently held feasts at each other's houses (where some of the members occasionally got a little out of control).[5] And instead of ritualistic sacrifices, they believed the only real sacrifice God wanted was their day-to-day devotion.[6] In addition, the early church ignored most of the racial, political, economic and gender prejudices of the day. Jews fellowshipped with Greeks, slaves with masters, rich with poor, and men with women.[7] It was downright scandalous. As the King James Version of the Bible says, the first Christians were a "peculiar people."[8] Or to put it another way, the early church was the counter-culture of their day.

But how did the church come about? Why did God create it and what is its purpose? This book will try to answer those questions and more. The book is divided into four parts. The first two parts will attempt to paint a picture of the church without filtering the text through the lens of man-made tradition. After all, our understanding of the Bible should be the basis of our traditions, not the other way around. In the third part of the book, I will contrast this picture with the church model we employ today, and, together, we will examine whether it complements or contradicts what the

---

5   **1 Corinthians 11:20, 21** For in eating, each one goes ahead with his own meal. One goes hungry, another gets drunk.

6   **Romans 12:1** I appeal to you therefore, brothers, by the mercies of God, to present your bodies as a living sacrifice, holy and acceptable to God, which is your spiritual worship.

7   **Galatians 3:28** There is neither Jew nor Greek, there is neither slave nor free, there is no male and female, for you are all one in Christ Jesus.

     James 1:9, 10 Let the lowly brother boast in his exaltation, and the rich in his humiliation …

8   **1 Peter 2:9** But ye are a chosen generation, a royal priesthood, an holy nation, a peculiar people … (KJV).

Bible says about church. And finally, in the fourth part of the book, we will take a brief look at church outside the box and discuss how to make the transition. Since the church is a spiritual community, we should probably start by looking at that first and most perfect spiritual community: God.

The Community of God

Our God is a mystery. He is three persons: the Father, Son and Holy Spirit. And those three persons compose one God. Our God is three-in-one. That means the persons of the Godhead are one in essence, substance, and nature; the Father is God, his Son Jesus Christ is God and the Holy Spirit is God. Yet they are also distinct from one another. We know they are distinct persons because the Bible makes this clear. For instance, when Jesus was baptized, all three members of the Godhead were present at one time, yet separate. Matthew 3:16, 17 tells us:

> And when Jesus was baptized, immediately he went up from the water, and behold, the heavens were opened to him, and he saw the Spirit of God descending like a dove and coming to rest on him; and behold, a voice from heaven said, "This is my beloved Son, with whom I am well pleased."

In these verses, we see Jesus here on earth, the Holy Spirit descending from heaven, and we hear God speaking from heaven, all at the same time. If God were simply a single being, how could he descend upon himself? And how could he be in heaven at the same time he was being baptized here on earth? Also, why would he talk to himself or call himself "son"?

Furthermore, Jesus made a clear distinction between himself and the Father, telling his disciples there was something only the Father knew.[1] Likewise, he made a distinction between himself and the Holy Spirit, saying people could be forgiven for speaking against the Son,

---

1   **Matthew 24:36** But concerning that day and hour no one knows, not even the angels of heaven, nor the Son, but the Father only.

but they could not be forgiven for speaking against the Holy Spirit.[2] Plus, he instructed his disciples to baptize new believers in the name of all three persons: the Father, the Son, and the Holy Spirit.[3]

Because the Godhead is three persons, we can rightly say our God is a spiritual community. And because God is perfect, we know the Godhead is the first and most perfect spiritual community. This means we can learn a lot about the way spiritual community functions based on the way the Godhead functions.

Perhaps the first thing we should examine is spiritual authority within the community of God. Man-made authority is often built on titles, positions, and hierarchy. A hierarchy is a system of persons or things ranked one above the other. Corporations and other organizations are hierarchies. But is that the way the Godhead is ordered? Is it like a chain-of-command where one member is in charge of the others? Are superiors and subordinates part of the natural order of spiritual community?

Jesus told his disciples he would send us the Holy Spirit.[4] We are also told gifts of the Holy Spirit are distributed according to God's will.[5] Based on verses like these, one could easily assume the Holy Spirit simply does the will of the Father and the Son and is, therefore, the lowest ranking member of the Godhead.

---

2   **Matthew 12:32** And whoever speaks a word against the Son of Man will be forgiven, but whoever speaks against the Holy Spirit will not be forgiven, either in this age or in the age to come.

3   **Matthew 28:19** Go therefore and make disciples of all nations, baptizing them in the name of the Father and of the Son and of the Holy Spirit …

4   **John 15:26** But when the Helper comes, whom I will send to you from the Father, the Spirit of truth, who proceeds from the Father, he will bear witness about me.

5   **Hebrews 2:4** God also bore witness by signs and wonders and various miracles and by gifts of the Holy Spirit distributed according to his will.

But we also established that people can be forgiven for speaking against the Son, but not for speaking against the Holy Spirit. That certainly makes it seem like the Holy Spirit has special significance in the Godhead. We also know Jesus was anointed with power that came from the Holy Spirit.[6] It was the Holy Spirit who sent Jesus into the desert to be tempted.[7] In verses such as these, the Holy Spirit is clearly not portrayed as a mere subordinate.

There are also plenty of verses that speak of Christ's obedience to the Father. Jesus said he came to do what the Father commanded him.[8] He said he could do nothing by himself, but only that which he saw the Father do.[9] He also told the disciples the Father was greater than he.[10] And before going to his death, Jesus surrendered his will to the Father and prayed, "Not my will, but yours, be done."[11] These verses definitely make it sound as if Jesus was subordinate to the Father.

But we are told plainly that Jesus was equal with his Father, yet chose to lay aside his divinity and become a servant for our sakes. Philippians 2:5–7 says:

---

6   **Acts 10:38** God anointed Jesus of Nazareth with the Holy Spirit and with power.

7   **Mark 1:12, 13** The Spirit immediately drove him out into the wilderness.

8   **John 14:31** But I do as the Father has commanded me …

9   **John 5:19** So Jesus said to them, "Truly, truly, I say to you, the Son can do nothing of his own accord, but only what he sees the Father doing. For whatever the Father does, that the Son does likewise."

10 **John 14:28** If you loved me, you would have rejoiced, because I am going to the Father, for the Father is greater than I.

11 **Luke 22:42** Father, if you are willing, remove this cup from me. Nevertheless, not my will, but yours, be done.

Have this mind among yourselves, which is yours in Christ Jesus, who, though he was in the form of God, did not count equality with God a thing to be grasped, but emptied himself, by taking the form of a servant, being born in the likeness of men.

Jesus chose to set aside his equality with God to become his servant here on earth. Similarly, he chose to become subject to Mary and Joseph when he was a child,[12] even though he was their Lord. Because of Christ's humility and obedience, he was later exalted to the place of preeminence. Philippians 2:9–11 tells us:

Therefore God has highly exalted him and bestowed on him the name that is above every name, so that at the name of Jesus every knee should bow, in heaven and on earth and under the earth, and every tongue confess that Jesus Christ is Lord, to the glory of God the Father.

As much as we might like to imagine the Godhead as a clearcut chain-of-command in which the Father gives the orders while the Son and Holy Spirit dutifully follow them, such a picture of the Godhead only holds up if we overemphasize certain scriptures and ignore others. The reality is: at times we see the Father or the Son dispatching the Holy Spirit to do certain works; at other times, we see the Holy Spirit empowering and directing the Son. We also know Christ laid aside his equality with God in order to become his servant here on earth; and we know God exalted him to the highest place for doing so.

12　**Luke 2:51** And he went down with them and came to Nazareth and was submissive to them.

That's not to say all members of the Godhead are equal in every way. But it seems careless to impose our man-made model of hierarchy onto the Godhead, since each of these three persons is solely focused on serving one another rather than ruling over one another. Moreover, such an oversimplification of the Godhead doesn't seem to take into account the fact that these three persons are also one.

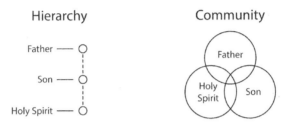

Jesus said plainly he and the Father are one.[13] He also said anyone who had seen him had seen the Father.[14] Additionally, Jesus is called *Immanuel*, which literally means "God with us." Likewise, Paul not only refers to Jesus as God,[15] but as the Spirit as well.[16] That certainly seems to blur the line between Christ and the Holy Spirit. Plus, we know Jesus was conceived of the Holy Spirit; yet he is known as the Son of God.[17] This infers that the Spirit and God are also one-and-the-same.

---

13 **John 10:30** I and the Father are one.

14 **John 14:9** Whoever has seen me has seen the Father.

15 **Titus 2:13** Waiting for our blessed hope, the appearing of the glory of our great God and Savior Jesus Christ...

16 **2 Corinthians 3:17** Now the Lord is the Spirit, and where the Spirit of the Lord is, there is freedom.

17 **Luke 1:35** And the angel answered her, "The Holy Spirit will come upon you, and the power of the Most High will overshadow you; therefore the child to be born will be called holy—the Son of God."

This oneness somewhat complicates our overly-simplistic picture of chain-of-command within the Godhead. Since the Father, Son, and Holy Spirit are one, any member of the Godhead who serves any other member is also serving himself. It is very reminiscent of how Paul told husbands to view their wives in Ephesians 5:28:

> In this same way, husbands ought to love their wives as their own bodies. He who loves his wife loves himself.

Later we will explore how the oneness experienced by a husband and wife is the perfect illustration of Christ and his church. But before we can do that, we need to finish examining the example of oneness we see expressed in the community of God. This oneness is so absolute, that it often blurs the lines between the individual members of the Godhead. The persons of the Godhead are so indivisible, that they sometimes appear to function collectively as a single person (or at least a group of persons with a single will). As an example, see how the Godhead expresses itself, referring to itself in the plural in Genesis 1:26:

> Then God said, "Let us make mankind in our image, in our likeness ..." (NIV).

This indivisible oneness is echoed in other Bible verses, such as when Paul calls Christ the visible image of the invisible God.[18] Or when he says Christ contains all the fullness of the Godhead in bodily form.[19] Jesus used a particular term to describe the type of

---

18 **Colossians 1:15** He is the image of the invisible God, the firstborn of all creation.

19 **Colossians 2:9** For in him the whole fullness of deity dwells bodily ...

oneness he has with God. He called it *complete unity*.[20] Although we can never fully comprehend complete unity, we can still learn from it. And, as we shall see later, we can actually experience it within the spiritual community known as the church. That's because the church is an extension of the community of God. But before we can discuss that, we need to look at God's original plan to extend the community of God.

---

20 **John 17:22, 23** I have given them the glory that you gave me, that they may be one as we are one— I in them and you in me—so that they may be brought to complete unity (NIV).

The Image of God

As discussed in the previous section, the desire to create mankind was shared among all the members of the Godhead; they had complete unity in this decision. Notice again how they speak in the plural in Genesis 1:26:

> Then God said, "Let us make mankind in our image,
> in our likeness ... " (NIV).

God desired objects of affection. The decision to make mankind was born out of the entire community of God in order to extend the community of God. We know we were created for community because we were created in the image of God, who is the first and most perfect spiritual community.

The story of the creation account begins with Genesis 1. On the first day, God created the heavens and the earth, the day and the night. At the end of the day, God saw that everything he created was good. This pattern repeats for days two, three, and so on. God creates the sky, the waters, the ground, the plants, and more. At the end of each day, he reflects on what he has made and declares it good. The creation account culminates with the sixth day and the creation of man. And for the first time, God realizes something in his creation is not good. Genesis 2:18 says:

> Then the Lord God said, "It is not good that the man
> should be alone; I will make him a helper fit for him."

In the perfect community of God, neither the Father, nor the Son, nor the Holy Spirit had ever been alone. Well, except for that moment when Jesus was separated from God during his redemptive work on the cross.¹ (Perhaps God, who exists outside of time, was actually remembering that moment when he said, "It is not good for the man to be alone.") Genesis 2:19–23 goes on to tell us:

> Now out of the ground the Lord God had formed every beast of the field and every bird of the heavens and brought them to the man to see what he would call them. And whatever the man called every living creature, that was its name. The man gave names to all livestock and to the birds of the heavens and to every beast of the field. But for Adam there was not found a helper fit for him. So the Lord God caused a deep sleep to fall upon the man, and while he slept took one of his ribs and closed up its place with flesh. And the rib that the Lord God had taken from the man he made into a woman and brought her to the man. Then the man said, "This at last is bone of my bones and flesh of my flesh; she shall be called Woman, because she was taken out of Man."

So God created a partner for Adam. Yet he did not form her the same way he formed Adam—directly from the clay. Possibly this was because he did not want to make Adam's partner a totally separate being. He did not want two distinct people that were merely alone together. He wanted them to truly be part of one another. Therefore, he formed woman from man. But how did God originally create men and women to function together? When God said he would make a *helper* for man, was he talking about a subordinate or an equal partner?

---

1   **Matthew 27:46** And about the ninth hour Jesus cried out with a loud voice, saying, "Eli, Eli, lema sabachthani?" that is, "My God, my God, why have you forsaken me?"

I am sure many will be quick to point out there are a handful of verses in the New Testament that seem to indicate men have authority over women. Rather than use our understanding of those verses as our lens to interpret the story of Adam and Eve, I would like to first examine the story of Adam and Eve to see if it can provide a better context for interpreting those other verses, which we can discuss later. After all, the creation story illustrates God's original intentions for men and women. Without a good grasp on God's original intentions, how can we ever hope to understand his ultimate intentions?

We might assume men are superior to women simply because the man was created first. But this doesn't seem consistent with the order of creation. God created the land before the plants in order to sustain the plants; God created the plants before the animals in order to sustain the animals; only after everything else was created did God create man. So it seems God created everything in order of least to greatest. Therefore, if men and women were not created equal, it would be more consistent with the order of creation to conclude women are superior to men since the woman came last, making her the pinnacle of creation.

Or we might assume men are superior to women because the man named the woman. We know that man was created to have authority over the animals; as a sign of his authority, he was allowed to name the animals. Therefore, isn't it a sign of men's headship over women that the man was the one who named his wife "woman?" There are a couple of problems with this theory. For one thing, Adam and Eve were both given authority over creation, including the animals. Genesis 1:28 explains this clearly:

And God blessed them. And God said to them, "Be fruitful and multiply and fill the earth and subdue it, and have dominion over the fish of the sea and over the birds of the heavens and over every living thing that moves on the earth."

Adam didn't name the animals by himself because he had more authority than his wife. His wife simply had not yet been created. Once woman was created, God charged the man and the woman to rule over the rest of creation together. This seems to imply men and women were created as partners. Further evidence of their equality is found in the verse in which God himself names the man and the woman, even though English translations of the Bible don't really reflect this. Genesis 5:2 says:

He created them male and female and blessed them. And he named them "mankind" when they were created (NIV).

The word we translate as "mankind" in this passage is actually the Hebrew word *adam*. Among its other uses, *adam* can mean "man," "men," "person," or "people." However, translators often choose to render it as a proper noun, giving us the name *Adam*. But in God's eyes, the man and woman were both *Adam*. Like the community of God, the original man and woman were distinct persons who were also one person. They were both created in the image of God; they were both created to rule over creation; and they could never be truly separated from one another. At least not until sin entered the world.

The Fall

Love isn't really love unless it is willingly given. This is one reason Adam and Eve were given the choice whether or not to love and obey God. As explained in Genesis 2:9 and 2:16, 17, their choice was symbolized in the form of two trees that stood in the heart of the Garden of Eden:

> And out of the ground the Lord God made to spring up every tree that is pleasant to the sight and good for food. The tree of life was in the midst of the garden, and the tree of the knowledge of good and evil. ... And the Lord God commanded the man, saying, "You may surely eat of every tree of the garden, but of the tree of the knowledge of good and evil you shall not eat, for in the day that you eat of it you shall surely die."

Knowledge   Life

Unfortunately, they were deceived and chose to eat from the tree of knowledge, allowing sin to enter the world. Because of sin, Adam and Eve were cast out of the garden—the place where they had previously walked and talked face-to-face with God.[1] Their sin

---

1   **Genesis 3:23** Therefore the Lord God sent him out from the garden of Eden to work the ground from which he was taken.

separated them from the community of God. This was the ultimate punishment for a people who were literally created to live in community with their Creator.

Not only did sin separate mankind from God, it separated mankind from one another. Because of sin, a curse was pronounced upon mankind. Several specifics are mentioned about the curse, but let's focus on one in particular. Genesis 3:16 says:

> To the woman he said ... "Your desire shall be for
> your husband, and he shall rule over you."

Before the Fall, mankind was given dominion over every living thing on the earth. But it was not until the Fall—until sin entered the world—that one person started ruling over another. Because of sin, Adam and Eve's relationship changed. Until this point in the story, the first husband and wife had simply been known as *man* and *woman*. Immediately after the curse is pronounced, Genesis 3:20 tells us:

> The man called his wife's name Eve, because she was
> the mother of all living.

For whatever reason, right after God pronounced the curse on mankind and right before they were banished from the garden, Adam chose to rename his wife. Sometimes, this verse is pulled out of context. It is presented as a beautiful moment where Adam honors his wife by declaring her the *Mother of All Living*. And if that is what Adam intended, we should not diminish such a beautiful act. Similarly, we cannot deny the honor that is rightfully Eve's as the mother of all.

However, we probably miss something when we take this verse out of context. From beginning to end, the entire chapter is about the fall of mankind. So we need to recognize that Adam renaming his wife was one of the very first acts of fallen man. Nowhere does the Bible say Adam made this decision as a result of the Fall. Perhaps Adam only did it to comfort and encourage his wife. Even though they had fallen from grace, he might have wanted to remind her she was still worthy of honor as the Mother of All Living.

Or perhaps Adam's view of his wife had become corrupted and he was now seeing her though the eyes of fallen man for the first time. It is quite possible he could only see her as the mother of his children now. That's not to say the Mother of All Living isn't a title of great esteem or that motherhood itself isn't an incredible honor. But this honor already belonged to Eve. God had already commanded the man and woman to be fruitful and multiply. The first woman was already destined to become the Mother of All Living, even before Adam recognized her as Eve.

The story of the Fall tells us a few things. First, since Adam began ruling over Eve as a direct result of sin, we can be confident this is not the way God originally created men and women to relate to one another. It was only because of sin that they became two truly separate people, alone together with conflicting ideas and competing agendas.[2] That meant one person would inevitably end up exerting his will over the other.

Second, if Adam actually diminished his wife's role in Genesis 3:20, it is possible he did so under the guise of honoring her. That doesn't

---

2   Although most translations of **Genesis 3:16** say something like, "Your desire shall be *for* your husband, and he shall rule over you," if you check the footnotes, some Bibles (such as the ESV) admit an equally valid interpretation of this verse is, "Your desire shall be *against* your husband, and he shall rule over you."

mean he was aware of this. It is very possible he did so under the self-deception of sin. Maybe he legitimately thought he was honoring her while at the same time he was actually diminishing her role from equal partner and fellow ruler. If so, we need to be wary so that we do not follow in his footsteps. As we shall see later, it is very important to recover how men and women were originally created to function together because it carries huge implications for the church.

Third, since Adam and Eve were created in the image of God, the way they originally related to each other must have been a direct reflection of the way the members of the Godhead relate to one another. And now that we know Adam and Eve didn't originally rule over one another, this further supports our original thesis that the members of the Godhead do not rule over one another either.

But why exactly did Adam and Eve's relationship change? Did sin simply corrupt their desire to mutually defer to each other? Or was it actually impossible for them to relate as equals since they could no longer experience spiritual unity? Is true unity with others no longer achievable once we become disconnected from God? If so, can mankind ever experience unity with their Creator and each other again?

Redemption

Undoubtedly, the most famous verse in all of Scripture is John 3:16:

> For God so loved the world, that he gave his only
> Son, that whoever believes in him should not perish
> but have eternal life.

This verse is truly beautiful, especially when you consider it is a direct quote from Jesus; he was talking about himself and foreshadowing the incredible sacrifice he was about to make for all of us. Mankind had its chance through Adam and Eve, but blew it. So Jesus came and willingly laid down his life to fix everything we messed up. That is why 1 Corinthians 15:45 and 15:47 refer to Jesus as "the last Adam":

> Thus it is written, "The first man Adam became a
> living being"; the last Adam became a life-giving
> spirit. ... The first man was from the earth, a man of
> dust; the second man is from heaven.

The Bible tells us the "first Adam" was a pattern for the Christ who would come later.[1] That is why it is so easy to see parallels between Adam and Eve and Christ and his church. For instance, no suitable mate could be found for Adam until God created one from the very substance of Adam himself. The same could be said of Christ and his Bride, the church.

In order to create Eve, God first placed Adam into a deep sleep.[2] Similarly, before the church was born, Christ was buried "asleep" in

---

1   **Romans 5:14** Adam, who was a type of the one who was to come.

2   **Genesis 2:21** So the Lord God caused a deep sleep to fall upon the man, and while he slept took one of his ribs and closed up its place with flesh.

the ground for three days.[3] God "wounded" Adam by taking part of his side and Christ was wounded for our transgressions.[4] On the cross, Christ was pierced in his side, out of which flowed both blood (atonement) and water (life).[5]

But perhaps the most important similarity can be found in Paul's letter to the church in Ephesus. The book of Ephesians opens by describing the church as the Body of Christ[6] and ends by describing the church as the Bride of Christ.[7] This is because the church is both the incarnation of Christ as well as his Bride. In this way, much like Adam and Eve were one, Jesus and his Bride are one. Paul even talks about this parallel in Ephesians 5:31, 32:

> "Therefore a man shall leave his father and mother
> and hold fast to his wife, and the two shall become
> one flesh." This mystery is profound, and I am saying
> that it refers to Christ and the church.

Much the way a groom longs to be one with his bride, we can hear how intensely Christ longed to be one with his own Bride, the church, while he was here on earth. In the Gospel of John,

---

3   **Matthew 12:40** For just as Jonah was three days and three nights in the belly of the great fish, so will the Son of Man be three days and three nights in the heart of the earth.

4   **1 Peter 2:24** He himself bore our sins in his body on the tree, that we might die to sin and live to righteousness. By his wounds you have been healed.

5   **John 19:34** But one of the soldiers pierced his side with a spear, and at once there came out blood and water.

6   **Ephesians 1:22, 23** And he put all things under his feet and gave him as head over all things to the church, which is his body ...

7   **Ephesians 5:25** Husbands, love your wives, as Christ loved the church and gave himself up for her ...

Jesus predicts his betrayal, foresees Peter's denial, and forewarns his disciples about his crucifixion. And right before his arrest, Jesus prays to the Father. It is a long, heartfelt prayer; it is the prayer of a man who knows this is the last time he will pray with his friends before going to his death. Therefore, it is very likely the request Jesus made during this prayer reflects the deepest desire of his heart.

And what was his heart's desire? *Oneness.* He prayed that we have oneness with each other and oneness with him. He prayed this for his own disciples and for every believer who would follow. This means oneness was Christ's heartfelt desire for his entire church. Three times he prayed for it: John 17:11, John 17:20, 21 and John 17:22, 23:

> Holy Father, protect them by the power of your name, the name you gave me, so that they may be one as we are one ... My prayer is not for them alone. I pray also for those who will believe in me through their message, that all of them may be one, Father, just as you are in me and I am in you ... I have given them the glory that you gave me, that they may be one as we are one—I in them and you in me—so that they may be brought to complete unity (NIV).

When Christ prayed for oneness a third time, he said the ultimate goal of our oneness should be *complete unity.* This type of oneness seems far beyond mere mortal cooperation and compromise. It sounds remarkably like the oneness shared among the members of the Godhead; the type of oneness shared by Adam and Eve before the Fall. Even though this specific prayer was about unity between believers (meaning the church), God's ultimate assignment for Christ was even more ambitious: to bring all creation back into unity with its Creator. As Ephesians 1:8–10 explains:

> With all wisdom and understanding, he made known to us the mystery of his will according to his good pleasure, which he purposed in Christ, to be put into effect when the times reach their fulfillment— to bring unity to all things in heaven and on earth under Christ.

The "last Adam" wasn't only sent to save souls. He came to restore everything that was corrupted when the "first Adam" allowed sin to enter the world. Not only did Christ die to save us from our sins, he died to undo the curse of sin entirely, as explained in Colossians 1:19, 20:

> For in him all the fullness of God was pleased to dwell, and through him to reconcile to himself all things, whether on earth or in heaven, making peace by the blood of his cross.

Christ sacrificed himself to reconcile all of creation to its Creator. And we are called to join him in this ministry of reconciliation.[8] Depending upon how big your view of God's grace is, this calling could take many forms. Obviously, there is the root of sin which must be confronted. But perhaps any good work that alleviates some portion of the effects of the curse could be considered a step toward the reconciliation of all things.

---

8   **2 Corinthians 5:18, 19** All this is from God, who through Christ reconciled us to himself and gave us the ministry of reconciliation; that is, in Christ God was reconciling the world to himself, not counting their trespasses against them, and entrusting to us the message of reconciliation.

We know toil, the pains of childbirth, and the subjugation of women were some of the consequences of the Fall.[9] Maybe anything we can do to alleviate these burdens could be considered a practical way of partnering with God in his larger work of reconciliation. That might include the invention of labor-saving technology, medical breakthroughs that alleviate the pains of childbirth, political and social initiatives for the advancement of women, and more.

However, as beautiful as these things are, the ultimate goal is the restoration of the unity we once had with each other and the unity we had with our Creator before the Fall. Incredibly, this unity is already available to us right now, through the church. But what does it look like for believers to have complete unity? Let's look at some examples from the early church. Specifically, let's look at the way the first church members shared their possessions, shared their spiritual gifts, and shared their faith.

---

9   **Genesis 3:16–19** To the woman he said, "I will surely multiply your pain in childbearing; in pain you shall bring forth children. Your desire shall be for your husband, and he shall rule over you." And to Adam he said, "Because you have listened to the voice of your wife and have eaten of the tree of which I commanded you, 'You shall not eat of it,' cursed is the ground because of you; in pain you shall eat of it all the days of your life; thorns and thistles it shall bring forth for you; and you shall eat the plants of the field. By the sweat of your face you shall eat bread, till you return to the ground, for out of it you were taken; for you are dust, and to dust you shall return."

Sharing Their Possessions

The story of the church begins in Acts 2. After the apostles were baptized with the Holy Spirit, Peter preached an amazing sermon. About 3,000 people were added to the faith and the church was born.[1] And only a couple of chapters later, the church began performing absolutely staggering acts of selflessness. Acts 4:32–35 tells us:

> Now the full number of those who believed were of one heart and soul, and no one said that any of the things that belonged to him was his own, but they had everything in common. And with great power the apostles were giving their testimony to the resurrection of the Lord Jesus, and great grace was upon them all. There was not a needy person among them, for as many as were owners of lands or houses sold them and brought the proceeds of what was sold and laid it at the apostles' feet, and it was distributed to each as any had need.

This was an astonishing feat, especially considering these people were brand new to the faith and Roman taxation was undoubtedly oppressive. Sadly, instead of imitating their example, we often hijack part of their story and distort it in order to compel today's congregations to give more money to organized churches. In Acts 5, we read about a husband and wife named Ananias and Sapphira. Like the believers who sold their lands and houses for the sake of the poor, this couple decided to sell a piece of property

---

1   **Acts 2:41** So those who received his word were baptized, and there were added that day about three thousand souls.

and hand the proceeds over to the church. However, they secretly held back some of the money and were promptly executed by the Holy Spirit.[2]

Even though this is an oft-quoted story in sermons and jokes about giving money to the church, Ananias and Sapphira's sin was not that they withheld some of their money; it was that they lied to the Holy Spirit about it.[3] Contrary to what you have heard in numerous Sunday morning sermons, New Testament believers are not required to give a tenth of their income (called a *tithe*) to the church. Tithing was only mandatory in the Old Testament, not the church. This is why there isn't a single command in the New Testament about tithing to the church. This is also why Peter told Ananias and Sapphira they were free to do whatever they wanted with their land and their money in Acts 5:4:

> Didn't it belong to you before it was sold? And after it was sold, wasn't the money at your disposal? What made you think of doing such a thing? You have not lied just to human beings but to God (NIV).

It is precisely this freedom that made the other believers' acts of generosity so commendable. Though generosity was encouraged and esteemed in the church, it was never obligatory. It was completely optional. As 2 Corinthians 9:7 says:

---

2   **Acts 5:5** When Ananias heard these words, he fell down and breathed his last.

    Acts 5:10 Immediately she fell down at his feet and breathed her last.

3   **Acts 5:3** But Peter said, "Ananias, why has Satan filled your heart to lie to the Holy Spirit and to keep back for yourself part of the proceeds of the land?"

Each one must give as he has decided in his heart, not reluctantly or under compulsion, for God loves a cheerful giver.

What motivated the members of the early church to give so generously wasn't obligation; it was revelation. As we shall see later, the early church enjoyed a supernatural unity that caused them to act as a single body. And because they realized they truly belonged to one another,[4] they felt compelled to take care of one another. As Paul says in 1 Corinthians 12:26:

If one member suffers, all suffer together; if one member is honored, all rejoice together.

This is why the ones who could give, gave, and the ones who needed, received. But the ones who could give definitely didn't do so reluctantly or under compulsion. In fact, in one instance, one of the poorer churches actually pleaded with Paul to let them give to help others who were even less fortunate.[5] Perhaps it helped that the early church knew they were giving money to people, not programs. They were not spending their hard-earned money on mere overhead expenses. Whenever you read about the early church collecting money, it was always to help the poor.[6]

---

4   **Romans 12:5** So in Christ we, though many, form one body, and each member belongs to all the others (NIV).

5   **2 Corinthians 8:3, 4** For they gave according to their means, as I can testify, and beyond their means, of their own accord, begging us earnestly for the favor of taking part in the relief of the saints …

6   **1 Corinthians 16:1** Now concerning the collection for the saints: as I directed the churches of Galatia, so you also are to do.

What a contrast we see between the early church and today's churches. In order to help the poor, the first thing the early church did was sell all their extra land and buildings. The first thing a church does today is buy extra land and buildings.

Sharing Their Gifts

Though God created the priesthood, it was never his long-term plan to relate to his children secondhand, through a small group of spiritual mediators. God always had another plan. As we noted earlier, Jeremiah 31:34 tells us God was looking forward to the day when he would have a one-on-one, personal relationship with each one of us:

> And no longer shall each one teach his neighbor and each his brother, saying, "Know the Lord," for they shall all know me, from the least of them to the greatest, declares the Lord.

In Exodus 19:6, even before he installed the tribe of Levi to serve as priests, he foreshadowed his ultimate intention to one day share the priesthood with all believers:

> And you shall be to me a kingdom of priests and a holy nation.

God's intention was finally realized with Christ's sacrifice on the cross, his resurrection, and the birth of the church. Jesus is now the High Priest who has bestowed a priesthood on all believers. As Hebrews 4:14–16 explains, we each now have access to God without the need for human mediators:

> Since then we have a great high priest who has passed through the heavens, Jesus, the Son of God … Let us then with confidence draw near to the throne of grace, that we may receive mercy and find grace to help in time of need.

This is why 1 Peter 2:5 says:

> You yourselves like living stones are being built up as a spiritual house, to be a holy priesthood, to offer spiritual sacrifices acceptable to God through Jesus Christ.

According to 1 Timothy 2:5, 6, Jesus our High Priest is now our sole mediator:

> For there is one God, and there is one mediator between God and men, the man Christ Jesus, who gave himself as a ransom for all ...

This is why 1 John 2:27 tells us:

> But the anointing that you received from him abides in you, and you have no need that anyone should teach you.

The realization of the priesthood of all believers radically redefined the way believers related to God and to one another. It was one of the most significant aspects of the early church. And it was evidenced in early church gatherings by the mutual participation of all church members. In 1 Corinthians 14:26 Paul describes the early church gathering:

> What then shall we say, brothers and sisters? When you come together, each of you has a hymn, or a word of instruction, a revelation, a tongue or an interpretation. Everything must be done so that the church may be built up (NIV).

In order for the church to be built up, each member had to exercise their calling as a fellow priest of the New Covenant. In many ways, an early church gathering was like a spiritual potluck. Rather than a single person bringing a sermon and everyone else sitting silently, listening to a lecture, each person brought something to share.

teachings   songs   stories   and more

Of course, the way each member exercised their calling depended upon their particular gift. Much like the various parts of our own physical bodies, the various members of the Body of Christ had different functions, as illustrated in Romans 12:4–8:

> For as in one body we have many members, and the members do not all have the same function, so we, though many, are one body in Christ, and individually members one of another. Having gifts that differ according to the grace given to us, let us use them: if prophecy, in proportion to our faith; if service, in our serving; the one who teaches, in his teaching; the one who exhorts, in his exhortation; the one who contributes, in generosity; the one who

leads, with zeal; the one who does acts of mercy, with cheerfulness.

Many of these gifts were not confined to the church. The vast majority of miracles we see performed in the book of Acts happened outside of church gatherings. However, it is abundantly clear that every church member was invited to exercise their spiritual gifts in church gatherings, as well. They were each expected to function as a fellow priest.

Rather than relegating all their religious duties to a select few, every believer was expected to instruct one another.[1] They were also expected to correct one another and minster to each other through psalms, hymns and spiritual songs.[2] And they were expected to confess their sins to each other, to pray, and to heal one another.[3]

Besides the fact many of today's churchgoers don't even discover their spiritual gifts, this level of participation is logistically impossible in today's large church gatherings. That is why so many institutional churches focus on getting everyone spiritually fed rather than giving everyone an opportunity to exercise their calling. Much like the rest of American culture, our churches seem to be suffering from an overabundance of eating, coupled with a complete lack of exercise.

---

1   **Romans 15:14** I myself am satisfied about you, my brothers, that you yourselves are full of goodness, filled with all knowledge and able to instruct one another.

2   **Colossians 3:16** Let the word of Christ dwell in you richly, teaching and admonishing one another in all wisdom, singing psalms and hymns and spiritual songs, with thankfulness in your hearts to God.

3   **James 5:16** Therefore, confess your sins to one another and pray for one another, that you may be healed. The prayer of a righteous person has great power as it is working.

Sharing Their Faith

In Matthew 18:20, Jesus promised his Spirit would be present whenever believers gather in his name:

> For where two or three are gathered in my name,
> there am I among them.

But isn't this redundant? Believers already have Christ in their hearts.[1] So why would we need at least one or two other believers for him to be present? Or was he talking about being present with us in a different way than he is present with individual believers?

If so, is it just a matter of numbers? Does merely having more believers in one place automatically add up to more of Christ in that place? Or was Jesus referring to something else when he said he would show up in a special way whenever we gather in his name?

Aren't we gathering in his name whenever we hold a church event? As long as Jesus is the subject of the sermon or the topic of the conversation or we have his name above the door and on our t-shirts, aren't we gathering in his name? Perhaps not. We must not forget there will be people who thought they performed miracles in his name, only to find out otherwise. Consider what Jesus says in Matthew 7:22, 23:

> Many will say to me on that day, "Lord, Lord, did
> we not prophesy in your name and in your name
> drive out demons and in your name perform many
> miracles?" Then I will tell them plainly, "I never knew
> you. Away from me, you evildoers!" (NIV).

---

1   **Colossians 1:27** To them God chose to make known how great among the Gentiles are the riches of the glory of this mystery, which is Christ in you, the hope of glory.

At no point does Jesus deny the fact that these people actually prophesied or drove out demons or performed miracles. That was not the issue. Their fatal mistake was that they never got to know him. Maybe we are never truly doing anything in his name if we are not doing it with him. As we already discussed, our God longs to be God-with-us. He does not want to give us a bunch of rules and regulations or even an arsenal of amazing spiritual gifts, but never get to know us until we meet up with him in eternity.

We delude ourselves if we think eternal life simply means not dying. That's perpetual existence, but it's not living. Eternal life is not a thing; it is a *person*. As Jesus says in John 17:3:

> And this is eternal life, that they know you the only
> true God, and Jesus Christ whom you have sent.

Simply making Christ our main topic of study without ever developing a real relationship with him is tragic. It is almost like attending lectures about swimming and mistaking the lectures for swimming lessons. We have to be on our guard against cultivating a false sense of relationship with the Lord.[2] Fans can sometimes develop a false sense of relationship with celebrities simply because they know so much about them. But real friends are more than just fans. And real disciples have an actual relationship with the Lord. They know his voice.[3] And when we come together collectively, something happens. Something is unlocked in the spirit and his Presence shows up in a profoundly different way. As an example, let's take another look at the story of the birth of the church.

---

2   **John 5:39, 40** You search the Scriptures because you think that in them you have eternal life; and it is they that bear witness about me, yet you refuse to come to me that you may have life.

3   **John 10:27** My sheep hear my voice, and I know them, and they follow me.

At the end of the Gospel of John, Jesus appears to his disciples after his resurrection. He then breathes on them and says, "Receive the Holy Spirit."[4] However, the Holy Spirit did not appear in that moment. And it wasn't just because Jesus had to return to the Father before he could send the Holy Spirit. This happened several days before the Holy Spirit finally appeared.[5]

So why the long wait? Perhaps there was something else that was required before the Holy Spirit could appear. Let's look at the setting right before the Holy Spirit arrives. Here is what Acts 2:1 says:

> And when the day of Pentecost was fully come, they were all with *one accord* in one place (KJV). (Italics added.)

The Greek word we translate as "one accord" is *homothumadon*. It means "having one mind, having the same passion, the same emotion, the same desire and purpose." It is a oneness beyond the natural. Does this sound like the oneness Jesus prayed for in John 17:11 and John 17:20–23? If so, it is probably no small thing that the Holy Spirit waited until the disciples were gathered in one accord, in complete unity, before he appeared and baptized them.

Similarly, after Peter was thrown into prison, the whole church came together and prayed ceaselessly for his release.[6] The night

---

4   **John 20:22** And when he had said this, he breathed on them and said to them, "Receive the Holy Spirit."

5   **Acts 1:5** You will be baptized with the Holy Spirit not many days from now.

6   **Acts 12:5** So Peter was kept in prison, but earnest prayer for him was made to God by the church.

before his trial, an angel appeared and released him.[7] This seems like another example of believers coming together in one accord and unlocking some kind of supernatural power. And as we noted earlier, the believers were also "of one heart and soul" when they became compelled to sell their lands and houses and completely wipe out poverty among them. This serves as another example of what is possible when believers have complete unity.

It probably shouldn't surprise us that coming together in complete unity creates the perfect conditions for God to show up in a uniquely powerful way. After all, complete unity is what he calls home; it is his natural habitat. And it is ours, as well. When we set aside all our competing agendas and our desires to control one another, and begin to remember how he originally created us to be—letting the lines between individuals become blurred until we finally become one—it makes him homesick for the type of community he had with us before the Fall. It fills him with longing to be with his Bride.

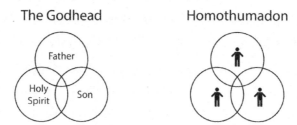

The Godhead — Homothumadon

And with his Presence comes power. In fact, there is so much supernatural power in our unity, it can actually convince unbelievers Jesus was sent from God! Jesus spoke of this in John 17:20, 21:

---

7 **Acts 12:7** And behold, an angel of the Lord stood next to him, and a light shone in the cell. He struck Peter on the side and woke him, saying, "Get up quickly." And the chains fell off his hands.

I do not ask for these only, but also for those who will believe in me through their word, that they may all be one, just as you, Father, are in me, and I in you, that they also may be in us, *so that the world may believe that you have sent me.* (Italics added.)

And he spoke of it again in John 17:23:

I in them and you in me, that they may become perfectly one, *so that the world may know that you sent me* and loved them even as you loved me. (Italics added.)

This is the key to how the early church "added to their number daily those who were being saved."[8] The secret to their success in evangelism was actually recorded, even though it is sometimes lost in translation. In the verse just prior to the one about their explosive growth, Acts 2:46 tell us:

And they, continuing daily with *one accord* ... (KJV). (Italics added.)

Just like on the Day of Pentecost, the believers in the early church were in one accord. Once again, the original Greek word used here is *homothumadon.* This means the early church was experiencing explosive growth for one reason—just as Jesus predicted, their complete unity drew unbelievers to the faith.

How exactly does this work? Complete unity (oneness) is what draws the Spirit, and his Presence draws others. It's that simple.

---

8   **Acts 2:47** And the Lord added to their number daily those who were being saved (NIV).

57

Rather than trying to get God to bless our work, we simply need to join him in his work. Instead of focusing on the world, trying to find better ways to market Christ to mankind, we simply need to focus on Christ until his Presence shows up and draws all mankind to himself.[9]

This might explain why God was so angry with Ananias and Sapphira; they were the first ones to break the bond of complete unity in the early church. By doing so, they were in danger of destroying the natural habitat that accommodates God's Presence. That's probably why they paid such a terrible price.

Of course, from their example, we might conclude it is much safer to simply keep God at a distance. Perhaps that is why we often choose to rely on expensive programs and time-consuming strategies in order to achieve what the early church seemed to accomplish so effortlessly. We can always control our man-made programs but we cannot control our God.

Sure, we now have vast menus of amazing church activities, entertaining events, targeted ministries, well-crafted sermons, flashy presentations, and professional pastors with impressive seminary degrees. But when an unbeliever walks into a church, is he hoping to witness spectacular music and dazzling productions and be won over by compelling arguments or is he looking for real evidence of the living God?

Shame on us if all we have are stories about the miraculous things God did for previous generations of believers, yet nothing but lame excuses for why he seems semi-retired today. Who could blame an unbeliever for turning around and walking away unconvinced? It was for this reason Paul urged us to seek the greater gifts. As he says in 1 Corinthians 14:24, 25:

---

9   **John 12:32** And I, when I am lifted up from the earth, will draw all people to myself.

But if all prophesy, and an unbeliever or outsider enters, he is convicted by all, he is called to account by all, the secrets of his heart are disclosed, and so, falling on his face, he will worship God and declare that God is really among you.

In fact, Paul seemed completely convinced a truly supernatural encounter with the Presence of God was absolutely necessary for producing an enduring faith. In 1 Corinthians 2:1–5 he explains:

And I, when I came to you, brothers, did not come proclaiming to you the testimony of God with lofty speech or wisdom. For I decided to know nothing among you except Jesus Christ and him crucified. And I was with you in weakness and in fear and much trembling, and my speech and my message were not in plausible words of wisdom, but in demonstration of the Spirit and of power, so that your faith might not rest in the wisdom of men but in the power of God.

So it seems when Christ said, "For where two or three are gathered in my name, there am I among them," he was indeed saying he would be present in his church in a uniquely powerful way. The longing of his heart is to be God-with-us, to be fully present in a profoundly supernatural way among his people. It is up to us whether or not we allow him to draw this close.

Part Two: Spiritual Parents

"There is nothing I like better than conversing with aged men. For I regard them as travelers who have gone a journey which I too may have to go, and of whom I ought to inquire whether the way is smooth and easy or rugged and difficult."

~ Socrates

Parents and Children

The word "Father" was rarely used to describe God in the Old Testament. Yet this was Christ's favorite way to describe God. He taught his disciples to think of God as their Father, as well. When they asked him how to pray, he told them to start with, "Our Father ..."[1] And once they embraced God as their Father, the disciples continued to speak of him this way throughout the rest of the New Testament.

The revelation of the relationship between the Father and the Son was so central to Christ's ministry that people actually had to be prepared in advance to receive it. Before Jesus was revealed in the flesh, John the Baptist was sent ahead to prepare the way. This is what Luke 1:17 says about John:

> And he will go on before the Lord, in the spirit and power of Elijah, to turn the hearts of the parents to their children and the disobedient to the wisdom of the righteous—to make ready a people prepared for the Lord (NIV).

In order to make people ready to receive the Lord, it stands to reason John needed to turn the disobedient to the wisdom of the righteous. But why did he need to turn the hearts of the parents to their children? Maybe we should look at the Godhead again to determine the answer.

Why are two members of the Godhead presented to us as Father and Son? Is it because the Father came first? Did the Father create the Son? No, we know that Jesus is as uncreated as his Father;

---

1   **Matthew 6:9** Our Father in heaven, hallowed be your name.

they have always existed together.[2] The distinction between the Father and Son does not occur to inform us which one existed first; they are equally eternal.

So then, is it to denote which one is superior, to show us who is in charge? No, because the Bible tells us plainly that Jesus had equality with God. Plus, if Jesus were not equal, that would mean he was not truly an adult son. Although a good son will always honor his father, adult sons do not relate to their fathers as subordinates to superiors; they relate as man-to-man.

Perhaps that perspective turns some of our church traditions head-over-heels. As we discussed earlier, we like to imagine the Godhead much like a man-made hierarchy. Possibly, we do this to justify adding man-made hierarchy to the church. Whatever the reason, we always seem to re-interpret the Father/Son relationship to be more like a Boss/Employee relationship.

Maybe the real reason they presented themselves to us as Father and Son is precisely *because* Jesus had equality with his Father. Perhaps they wanted to set an example for all parents, modeling the ultimate goal of every parent/child relationship: to arrive at the place where parents and children become peers. If so, this might explain why John had to prepare the way by turning the hearts of the parents to their children: to prepare the people for a revelation of a Parent/Child relationship that would become the foundation for all spiritual leadership in the church.

We already established the church is an extension of the community of God and the example of perfect spiritual community for the church. Since the relationship between a Father and Son is at the heart of the community of God, should we find it surprising the relationship between spiritual parents and spiritual children is at the heart of the church?

---

2   **John 1:1** In the beginning was the Word, and the Word was with God, and the Word was God.

Fathers and Mothers

In order to be eligible for a job, you must meet certain requirements. To work in an accounting department, you may need proficiency in both math and Excel. To deliver pizza, you may need a driver's license and your own car. In each instance, the requirements for the job tell you something about the job itself. Even without any prior knowledge about a particular job, the specific duties can be fairly-well grasped based on the requirements alone.

What does this have to do with the church? Well, we know the early church had overseers. However, our ideas about their exact function have changed over time, and the original purpose of overseers has become obscured by church tradition. So let's see if we can figure out their original function by looking at the job requirements. In 1 Timothy 3:1–7, Paul tells us:

> Here is a trustworthy saying: Whoever aspires to be an overseer desires a noble task. Now the overseer is to be above reproach, faithful to his wife, temperate, self-controlled, respectable, hospitable, able to teach, not given to drunkenness, not violent but gentle, not quarrelsome, not a lover of money. He must manage his own family well and see that his children obey him, and he must do so in a manner worthy of full respect. (If anyone does not know how to manage his own family, how can he take care of God's church?) He must not be a recent convert, or he may become conceited and fall under the same judgment as the devil. He must also have a good reputation with outsiders, so that he will not fall into disgrace and into the devil's trap (NIV).

There has been a lot of debate over the years as to whether or not women can be overseers. One big hangup is the fact that this passage seems to describe only men. But that is mostly due to inaccurate translations, plus years of church tradition, which also influenced our translations. In the original Greek text, no masculine pronouns appear in this passage. (Nor are there any masculine pronouns in the list of requirements in Titus 1:5–9.)

Therefore, instead of translating these verses using purely masculine pronouns like *he*, it might have made more sense to use gender-neutral substitutes like *this person*. In this way, our English translations would not add a gender bias that was not there in the original Greek. Perhaps this passage should read:

> Whoever aspires to be an overseer desires a noble task. … *This person* must manage their own family well and see that their children obey them, and *this person* must do so in a manner worthy of full respect. … (Italics added.)

The only requirement for overseers that is specifically directed toward men is the requirement for overseers to be faithful to their wives. Because of this, translators often assumed this entire passage is specifically directed toward men. But it is equally possible this one requirement was specifically directed to the male overseers and the rest of the requirements were directed toward both men and women.

If the early church did allow for both men and women overseers, it makes sense the male overseers would need such a requirement. The first century was decidedly misogynistic. Men could have multiple wives but women could not have multiple husbands.[1] Only husbands

---

1   **1 Kings 11:3** He had 700 wives, who were princesses, and 300 concubines.

could issue a certificate of divorce, not their wives.[2] Not to mention John 8 tells the story of a woman caught in the act of adultery; she and the man she was with were both caught, yet only the woman was in danger of being put to death.[3]

Also, if we insist women cannot be overseers because of a strict interpretation of the verse about overseers' wives, then we need to be consistent. Since single men do not have wives, they must be disqualified from being overseers as well. Furthermore, when we simply use this verse as a proof text for determining the gender of overseers, it is possible we miss the real purpose of this verse.

The requirement for an overseer to be faithful to his wife also meant having only one wife. This meant treating wives more like partners than property, which sounds a lot like the ministry of reconciliation at work. In such a misogynistic culture, this was a big step toward restoring the original order between husbands and wives—two members becoming one flesh and relating as equals.

Such a decree seems very counter-culture for its day. In light of this, isn't it tragic to think a passage probably intended to help restore equality is now being used to accomplish the exact opposite? This may be a controversial interpretation in many churches today but, as we shall see later, it's not unfounded. For now, it's enough to simply introduce the possibility. In the meantime, let's return to figuring out the actual function of an overseer.

As previously stated, our ideas about overseers have changed. In many church traditions, the overseer has become an office that is

---

2   **Matthew 19:8** He said to them, "Because of your hardness of heart Moses allowed you to divorce your wives, but from the beginning it was not so."

3   **John 8:3–5** The scribes and the Pharisees brought a woman who had been caught in adultery, and placing her in the midst they said to him, "Teacher, this woman has been caught in the act of adultery. Now in the Law Moses commanded us to stone such women. So what do you say?"

largely administrative. This is very interesting considering the gift of administration is not listed in the requirements for overseers, even though Paul knew about this gift and talked about it in 1 Corinthians 12:28.[4] (Some translations call it *guidance* instead of *administrating*.) If anything, the requirements for overseers seem to focus on how prospective overseers treat their families. If our assumption about job requirements is correct, then we might conclude overseers are simply intended to be spiritual parents.

That seems consistent with the perspective of the apostles. Over and over in the New Testament, they refer to the believers in the early churches as their children, not just children of God but their own children. This parent/child language is so prevalent in their letters, it is clear the apostles truly believed they had some kind of parental responsibility toward the early churches. The following verses are just a small sampling of the many passages that illustrate this:

> 1 Corinthians 4:14; 2 Corinthians 12:14; Galatians 4:19; 1 Thessalonians 2:11, 12; 1 John 2:28; 1 John 3:18; and 3 John 4.[5]

---

4   **1 Corinthians 12:28** And God has appointed in the church first apostles, second prophets, third teachers, then miracles, then gifts of healing, helping, administrating, and various kinds of tongues.

5   **1 Corinthians 4:14** I do not write these things to make you ashamed, but to admonish you as my beloved children.

2 Corinthians 12:14 Here for the third time I am ready to come to you. And I will not be a burden, for I seek not what is yours but you. For children are not obligated to save up for their parents, but parents for their children.

Galatians 4:19 My little children, for whom I am again in the anguish of childbirth until Christ is formed in you!

1 Thessalonians 2:11, 12 For you know how, like a father with his children, we exhorted each one of you and encouraged you and charged you to walk in a manner worthy of God, who calls you into his own kingdom and glory.

Also, Paul speaks of his disciples Timothy and Titus (as well as Onesimus) as if they were his own biological children. Likewise, Peter speaks the exact same way about his disciple Mark. Just look at:

> 1 Corinthians 4:17; 1 Timothy 1:2; Titus 1:4; Philemon 10; and 1 Peter 5:13.[6]

The significance of this parental perspective cannot be overemphasized. For one thing, parents teach by being living examples, through walking day-by-day alongside their children. Therefore, it makes sense that true, spiritual parents must walk day-by-day alongside their spiritual children, as well.

Jesus set the pattern with his own disciples, sharing every aspect of his everyday life with them: working, eating, hanging out together at all hours. And the apostles followed this same pattern. Notice how Paul describes his discipleship of Timothy in Philippians 2:22:

---

1 John 2:28 And now, little children, abide in him, so that when he appears we may have confidence and not shrink from him in shame at his coming.

1 John 3:18 Little children, let us not love in word or talk but in deed and in truth.

3 John 4 I have no greater joy than to hear that my children are walking in the truth.

6   1 Corinthians 4:17 That is why I sent you Timothy, my beloved and faithful child in the Lord ...

1 Timothy 1:2 To Timothy, my true child in the faith ...

Titus 1:4 To Titus, my true child in a common faith ...

Philemon 10 I appeal to you for my child, Onesimus, whose father I became in my imprisonment.

1 Peter 5:13 She who is at Babylon, who is likewise chosen, sends you greetings, and so does Mark, my son.

> But you know Timothy's proven worth, how as a son
> with a father he has served with me in the gospel.

While Paul was discipling Timothy, they worked side-by-side; they shared day-to-day life together. This is how Jesus intended discipleship to work and why Hebrews 13:7 says:

> Remember your leaders, those who spoke to you the
> word of God. Consider the outcome of their way of
> life, and imitate their faith.

How can we know our leaders' way of life to such a degree that we can imitate them, unless we are a part of their daily lives? Curated stories about someone's life, delivered from behind a pulpit, cannot give us enough access to truly imitate a person or provide enough insight to know whether or not they are worth imitating. This is probably why Peter used the analogy of shepherds when he instructed the church elders. In 1 Peter 5:2, 3 he says:

> Be shepherds of God's flock that is under your
> care, watching over them—not because you must,
> but because you are willing, as God wants you to
> be; not pursuing dishonest gain, but eager to serve;
> not lording it over those entrusted to you, but being
> examples to the flock (NIV).

In order to become true examples to the flock, elders were to live like shepherds. As the saying goes, "real shepherds smell like sheep." Meaning, true spiritual shepherds live day-by-day alongside their sheep just like the actual shepherds we read about in Luke 2:8:

And in the same region there were shepherds out in
the field, keeping watch over their flock by night.

This is not to say we cannot learn something from Sunday
morning sermons, even if we have no personal relationship with the
pastor. However, this should be known as teaching or preaching, not
discipleship or pastoring. Those latter terms imply we are living a
shared spiritual life, which is simply not the case with someone we
see only once a week, standing on a platform.

Based on the requirements we find in Scripture, we now know
the original overseers were not church administrators who held some
kind of office; they were spiritual parents who lived day-by-day
alongside their spiritual children like shepherds (not unlike Jesus,
the Good Shepherd).[7] The original overseers were relational, not
positional. But what about elders, bishops, presbyters, and pastors?
How do they fit into the overall picture of spiritual parenting?

---

7   **John 10:14** I am the good shepherd. I know my own and my own know me ...

One Set of Parents

Most of today's churches seem to operate as religious organizations run by people in various positions such as deacons, elders and pastors. These different church offices are ranked one above the other in an organizational hierarchy. We have been taught these positions come from Scripture. And indeed you can find words such as "deacon," "elder," and "pastor" in many of the biblical descriptions of the early church.

But because today's churches operate more as organizations, we tend to read the Bible through an organizational lens. This is why we do not notice the disconnect between the early church and today's churches, especially when it comes to titles and positions. Much like the community of God, each member of the early church willingly served the other members.[1] Yes, there were spiritual leaders, but there was absolutely no organizational hierarchy.

To prove this, we need to dispel a common myth about church leadership. Specifically, we need to do away with the idea that bishops, presbyters, overseers, elders, and pastors were separate persons. These were not separate people; they were different terms for a single group of people. These terms denote the spiritual parents we read about in the previous section. Most of the time, these leaders were simply called *elders*. And they were eventually appointed in all of the churches, as seen in Acts 14:23:

> And when they had appointed elders for them in
> every church, with prayer and fasting they committed
> them to the Lord in whom they had believed.

---

1   **Philippians 2:3, 4** Do nothing from selfish ambition or conceit, but in humility count others more significant than yourselves. Let each of you look not only to his own interests, but also to the interests of others.

To get a better understanding of elders, let's start with the word "elder" itself, which is a translation of the Greek word *presbýteros*. This word was used over 60 times in the original Greek version of the New Testament. *Presbýteros* means "one who is mature, having seasoned judgment and experience." The word was used to describe both mature men and mature women. The only way to determine the intended gender of a specific use is through context. For instance, many English translations of 1 Timothy 5:1, 2 say:

> Do not rebuke an older man but encourage him as you would a father, younger men as brothers, older women as mothers, younger women as sisters, in all purity.

The original Greek text of this verse used the word *presbýteros* twice: once for *older man* and once for *older women*. Yet translators are able to differentiate the genders because of context. Paul tells us to treat one *presbýteros* as a "father" and the other as "mothers."

However, translators also added a certain degree of confusion by translating *presbýteros* as "older man" and "older women" in this verse, yet translating the word as "elder" or "elders" nearly everywhere else. By doing this, they separated this particular verse about men and women elders from all the other verses about elders, supporting the assumption there were no women elders in the early church. But let's forge ahead and see what else we can uncover about elders.

The Greek word for shepherd is *poimén* and the Greek word for overseer is *episkopos*. In the New Testament, these terms illustrate different functions but they do not connote separate persons. Jesus was referred to as both our "Shepherd" and "Overseer."[2] Likewise, in Acts 20:28, Paul instructs the elders of the church to be both shepherds and overseers, saying:

> Keep watch over yourselves and all the flock of which
> the Holy Spirit has made you overseers. Be shepherds
> of the church of God, which he bought with his own
> blood (NIV).

Furthermore, the word "bishop" is simply the English translation of the Greek word *episkopos*. Therefore, elders, presbyters, shepherds, overseers, and bishops all refer to the same group of people. In the early church, there would have been no such thing as a bishop that was somehow separate from an elder.

However, things get even more interesting with the Greek word for "shepherd" we saw just a moment ago, *poimén*. As we noted above, Paul instructed the elders to be both overseers and shepherds. Likewise, Peter refers to elders as shepherds in 1 Peter 5:1, 2:

> To the elders among you ... Be shepherds of God's
> flock that is under your care, watching over them—not
> because you must, but because you are willing ... (NIV).

Whenever the Bible talks about spiritual shepherds in the early church, it is always talking about elders. And the only time the word *poimén* is translated as anything other than "shepherd" is in Ephesians 4:11, where it is translated as "pastor" instead:

---

2   **1 Peter 2:25** For you were straying like sheep, but have now returned to the
Shepherd and Overseer of your souls.

> So Christ himself gave the apostles, the prophets, the evangelists, the *pastors* and teachers ... (NIV). (Italics added.)

This single aberrant translation of the word *poimén* has caused a whirlwind of confusion in the church. This is the one and only time the English word "pastor" appears in most popular translations of the Bible. And there is no good reason to translate the word any differently in this instance. (Plus, the English word "pastor" actually means "shepherd", anyway. So nothing is gained by using a different word.) It is abundantly clear the elders were the only shepherds in the early church. Yet this one bizarre translation of the word *poimén* has disconnected it from all other uses of the exact same word, setting the imaginary "pastor" apart from (and often higher than) the other elders.

The big takeaway from realizing bishops, presbyters, overseers, elders, and pastors were one-in-the-same isn't that there was one single position in the early church; it's that there were *no positions* in the early church! As we shall see, functioning as an elder is relational, not positional. The early church did not have titles and positions; they simply had spiritual parents.

The early church's spiritual parents were known as:

Elders	Also called presbyters
Shepherds	Also called pastors
Overseers	Also called bishops

That only strengthens the case for female elders since it is highly unlikely the church was meant to function with only spiritual fathers and no spiritual mothers. Remember, God had already declared he would one day pour out his Spirit in a profoundly new way on both men and women. Joel 2:28, 29 says:

> And it shall come to pass afterward, that I will pour out my Spirit on all flesh; your sons and your daughters shall prophesy, your old men shall dream dreams, and your young men shall see visions. Even on the male and female servants in those days I will pour out my Spirit.

Peter said this prophecy was fulfilled with the birth of the church.[3] Prior to this, only men could be priests. But the church was to become the fulfillment of God's desire to have a nation of priests, a priesthood of all believers.[4] How can today's churches rightly call themselves a priesthood of all believers if the priesthood is only available to half their people? But let's get back to the discussion about leadership positions in the church.

If you read through the book of Acts with fresh eyes rather than filtering the text through the lens of tradition, you will quickly discover the elders (also called presbyters) were the sole shepherds (also called pastors) and overseers (also called bishops) of the early church. These elders were a reflection of the Father, meaning they were more like spiritual parents than administrators.

Therefore, claiming our present organizational hierarchy comes from the Bible simply doesn't hold water. Yes, today's churches use

---

3 **Acts 2:16, 17** But this is what was uttered through the prophet Joel …

4 **Exodus 19:6** And you shall be to me a kingdom of priests and a holy nation.
   1 Peter 2:9 But you are a chosen race, a royal priesthood …
   Revelation 1:6 And made us a kingdom, priests to his God and Father …

many of the same words we find in Scripture such as "deacon," "elder," and "pastor." But we have completely redefined these words to fit our man-made, church model.

However, we haven't talked specifically about deacons yet. Aren't there scriptures that substantiate deacons are subordinate to elders? And if so, doesn't the relationship between elders and deacons prove there is actually some degree of spiritual hierarchy in the church?

Imaginary Positions

We have already dispelled most of the myths about church positions and titles, as well as the myth of the stand-alone senior pastor. But what about deacons? As we read through the history of the early church in the book of Acts, we come across a story in chapter 6 in which the church was having a problem with the distribution of food. In Acts 6:2–4, the apostles came up with this solution:

> And the twelve summoned the full number of the disciples and said, "It is not right that we should give up preaching the word of God to serve tables. Therefore, brothers, pick out from among you seven men of good repute, full of the Spirit and of wisdom, whom we will appoint to this duty. But we will devote ourselves to prayer and to the ministry of the word."

Some readers seem to believe the apostles had more important things to do than wait on tables. According to this interpretation, they needed subordinates to take care of the less spiritual tasks while they focused on more spiritual duties, like praying and preaching. Considering Jesus had recently washed their feet like a common house servant and told them to follow his example,[1] that interpretation is extremely unlikely.

Tradition tells us the seven men that were selected were the first church deacons, even though that word is never actually used in this particular passage. Most of what we know about deacons comes from Paul's first letter to Timothy. Right after Paul lays out the requirements for overseers, 1 Timothy 3:8–13 goes on to say:

---

1 **John 13:15** For I have given you an example, that you also should do just as I have done to you.

In the same way, deacons are to be worthy of respect, sincere, not indulging in much wine, and not pursuing dishonest gain. They must keep hold of the deep truths of the faith with a clear conscience. They must first be tested; and then if there is nothing against them, let them serve as deacons. In the same way, the women are to be worthy of respect, not malicious talkers but temperate and trustworthy in everything. A deacon must be faithful to his wife and must manage his children and his household well. Those who have served well gain an excellent standing and great assurance in their faith in Christ Jesus (NIV).

This list follows the same pattern as the previous list about overseers: no masculine pronouns were used in the original Greek to describe deacons, yet there is a requirement for deacons to be faithful to their wives, just like overseers. But whereas that single requirement has often been used to assert the entire passage about overseers was directed toward men, it is much more problematic to say the same for this passage.

For one thing, many translators believe Paul's comment, "In the same way, the women . . ." could also be translated, "In the same way, female deacons . . ." But even more problematic is the fact that Paul, the same person who wrote both these lists of requirements, blatantly mentions a female deacon in Romans 16:1:

I commend to you our sister Phoebe, a deacon of the church in Cenchreae (NIV).

But how could Phoebe be a deacon in the early church if deacons were required to be faithful to their wives and therefore, must have been married men? She couldn't, unless it was understood the requirement about deacons' wives was directed to the male deacons and all the other requirements were directed toward both men and women. But once we admit this, it leaves a gaping hole in the argument against women overseers.

How can we concede the list of requirements for deacons was directed at both men and women without admitting the same for the list of requirements for overseers? Plus, we already established overseers are elders. And we also established the original Greek word for "elder" was used for both older men and older women.

Furthermore, the whole debate over whether women can hold positions of leadership stems from the false assumption that there actually *are* leadership positions in the church. We saw how church tradition separated the terms elder, bishop, shepherd, presbyter, overseer, and pastor into distinct, imaginary positions. So, should we be surprised to discover there was no such thing as a "deacon" in the early church?

Our word "deacon" comes from the Greek word *diakonos* which appears 29 times in the New Testament. However, it is only translated as "deacon" about 5 times, just enough to give this imaginary position some legitimacy. But the word *diakonos* actually means "servant." It is the word Jesus used in regard to the apostles in Mark 10:42–44:

> And Jesus called them to him and said to them, "You know that those who are considered rulers of the Gentiles lord it over them, and their great ones exercise authority over them. But it shall not be so among you. But whoever would be great among you must be your *servant,* and whoever would be first among you must be slave of all. (Italics added.)

And it is the same word the apostle Paul often used to describe himself. As an example, take Ephesians 3:7:

> I became a *servant* of this gospel by the gift of God's grace given me through the working of his power (NIV). (Italics added.)

And it is the exact same word used to describe Christ in Romans 15:8:

> For I tell you that Christ has become a *servant* of the Jews on behalf of God's truth ... (NIV). (Italics added.)

The word *diakonos* was simply used to describe anyone who serves, not reserved for a select group of people who held some kind of official position in the church. However, the church had already become an institution by the time the Bible was translated. Therefore, the organizational perspective of the translators colored their interpretation of the texts to help them justify man-made positions such as pastors, bishops, and deacons. Not to mention the insertion of decidedly male pronouns ensured these positions could only be occupied by men. Yet this does raise an interesting question: if the church is not an organization and the servants described in 1 Timothy do not hold actual positions in the church, then why is there a list of requirements to be met in order to be recognized as servants in the church?

Because these members assume certain responsibilities for the church, they must be trustworthy and responsible. Therefore they must meet a certain standard. Put simply, a *diakonos* is any reliable, mature member, other than an elder, who agrees to take on certain responsibilities for the church. It is not unlike the way older children take on household chores in order to lift some of the burden off mom and dad.

We know one of the spiritual gifts Paul talked about was the gift of administration. But that doesn't mean the early church itself was an administration. There is always a certain amount of business to be done within a family. But doing business doesn't automatically make you a business. And organizing doesn't have to turn you into an organization.

When the apostles said, "It is not right that we should give up preaching the word of God to serve tables," they were not saying, "This task is beneath us; give this menial labor to someone less important." They were saying, "We know what we're good at; we'll stick to that. Find a few other people who can do this other task well." And seven responsible church members stepped up to serve.

But they did not become "deacons," having positions of authority somewhere above the average church member, but still lower than an elder (like some kind of spiritual middle-managers). That model comes from corporate America; it has nothing to do with genuine church community. In the first churches, there were simply seniors and juniors, shepherds and sheep, parents and children, a simple reflection of the Father and Son.

So now we have reconciled bishops, presbyters, overseers, and pastors into a single mature group of men and women, having seasoned judgment and experience, known as "elders." We also know there were servants (who were not elders) who took on certain responsibilities for the church. But how should we understand apostles, prophets, evangelists, and teachers?

Ephesians 4

In most English translations of the Bible, the word "pastor" is used only once, in Ephesians 4:11. We have already established that the elders were the "pastors" spoken of in this verse. However, four other persons are mentioned in this passage as well: apostles, prophets, evangelists, and teachers. Who are these people and what is their exact function in the church?

Many of our current church traditions interpret this passage as a list of church leaders, with the pastor as the preeminent leader in the list. But that is simply not the way these persons are described in this passage. Ephesians 4:11–13 tells us these church members are equippers:

> So Christ himself gave the apostles, the prophets, the evangelists, the pastors and teachers, to equip his people for works of service, so that the body of Christ may be built up until we all reach unity in the faith and in the knowledge of the Son of God and become mature, attaining to the whole measure of the fullness of Christ (NIV).

The persons mentioned in this list are specifically called to equip the rest of the church for ministry. But that could mean one of two things: either they equip the rest of the church *using* their particular spiritual gifts, or they equip the rest of the church *to use* their particular spiritual gifts. (If you missed it, read that last sentence again.) It might take an illustration to explain the difference.

Let's take a scene from a typical Sunday morning church service. You have a church member with a gift of teaching, usually known as a pastor, who teaches weekly sermons while the rest of the congregation simply sits and listens. Let's say this week's sermon is about forgiveness and the application is very practical. One might say this pastor is equipping his congregation to exercise forgiveness. Using this interpretation of Ephesians 4:11–13, the pastor equips the rest of the church by teaching the practical application of Scripture.

However, a very different interpretation of this passage would be that a church member with the gift of teaching is supposed to teach the rest of the congregation how to teach. Just as we learn math from a math teacher and history from a history teacher, church members can learn to teach from a teacher, to evangelize from an evangelist, to prophesy from a prophet, and so on. In this interpretation of Ephesians 4:11–13, the members mentioned in this list use their gifts to equip the rest of the church to do these ministries, not simply doing these ministries for them.

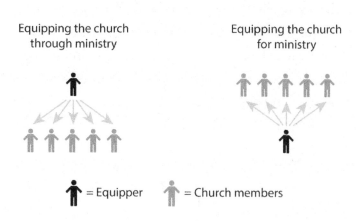

The latter interpretation is radically different from the former because it takes the ministries of the church out of the hands of a select few and places them into the hands of the priesthood of all believers. That's not to say the church members who specialize in these gifts don't perform these ministries, as well. But they do so alongside the rest of the congregation, the way Jesus did with his own disciples, with the goal of teaching the whole church how to perform these ministries.

Though this interpretation is at odds with our current church model, the original expectation was for every church member to teach, prophesy, pastor, evangelize, and play a part in the apostolic work of the early church. Consider how the writer of Hebrews rebuked that particular church because the entire congregation had not yet become teachers. Hebrews 5:12 says:

> In fact, though by this time you ought to be teachers, you need someone to teach you the elementary truths of God's word all over again. You need milk, not solid food! (NIV).

If the expectation was for everyone to teach, it makes sense that a church member with a specialization in teaching could have helped equip them to teach. And much like the writer of Hebrews expected everyone in the church to teach, Paul wanted everyone in the church to prophesy. In 1 Corinthians 14:5 he says:

> Now I want you all to speak in tongues, but even more to prophesy.

We know his desire was for the entire church.[1] So, why would Paul encourage the whole congregation to seek the gift of prophecy if it were only available to a handful of designated prophets?

Likewise, why were early church members expected to perform so many of the functions we now assign to professional pastors?

---

1   1 Corinthians 14:1 Pursue love, and earnestly desire the spiritual gifts, especially that you may prophesy.

In a previous section, we saw how believers in the early church were expected to instruct one another, correct one another, minister to one another through psalms, hymns and spiritual songs, confess their sins to one another, pray for one another, and heal one another.

Obviously, the average church member might not perform some ministries to the same degree as the persons mentioned in Ephesians 4:11–13 who specialize in certain gifts. But then again, a math professor would not expect every math student to become a fellow math professor. This is why the Word only asks us to prophesy in proportion to our faith.[2] The question at hand is: does the Word expect everyone in the church to exercise these gifts to some degree?

So far, it certainly seems that way. We already have a solid case for each church member being expected to teach, prophesy, and pastor. Now let's talk about apostles. One of the main functions of an apostle is church planting. But would it be practical for every church member to go out and plant churches? No. If everyone in the congregation were sent out, there would be no congregation left. So, how can each church member participate in this ministry?

There are numerous references in the New Testament to various people who assisted Paul on his missions to plant churches. (Romans 16:21, 2 Corinthians 8:23, Philemon 1:23, 24 are just a few examples.)[3] Also, the early churches financially supported his

---

2 **Romans 12:6–8** Having gifts that differ according to the grace given to us, let us use them: if prophecy, in proportion to our faith …

3 **Romans 16:21** Timothy, my fellow worker, greets you; so do Lucius and Jason and Sosipater, my kinsmen.

2 Corinthians 8:23 As for Titus, he is my partner and fellow worker for your benefit. And as for our brothers, they are messengers of the churches, the glory of Christ.

ministry efforts. As an example, consider how the church at Philippi sent Paul financial support while he was ministering in Thessalonica.[4] This is why Paul refers to the Philippians as his ministry partners in Philippians 1:4, 5:

> In all my prayers for all of you, I always pray with joy because of your partnership in the gospel from the first day until now ... (NIV).

In a very real sense, apostolic ministry is a ministry of the church, not just the handful of individuals who are sent out to do the actual church planting.

But what about evangelism? The term "evangelist" can be problematic because the specific word is used only three times in the entire Bible (one of them being Ephesians 4:11–13). However, we know the gift of evangelism is about proclaiming the Gospel and winning souls. And Paul certainly had that gift. Interestingly, he referred to proclaiming the Gospel as a "priestly duty."[5] Since every believer is a priest, wouldn't this imply all believers are supposed to perform this duty?

Also we know Peter was an evangelist. Remember what happened in Acts 2:41 after Peter preached to the crowds:

Philemon 1:23, 24 Epaphras, my fellow prisoner in Christ Jesus, sends greetings to you, and so do Mark, Aristarchus, Demas, and Luke, my fellow workers.

4   **Philippians 4:16** Even in Thessalonica you sent me help for my needs once and again.

5   **Romans 15:16** He gave me the priestly duty of proclaiming the gospel of God ... (NIV).

> So those who received his word were baptized, and
> there were added that day about three thousand souls.

Surely, Peter should be able to teach us something about evangelism. In 1 Peter 3:15 he says:

> Always be prepared to give an answer to everyone
> who asks you to give the reason for the hope that
> you have.

Peter did not expect every one of us to evangelize as effectively as someone with the gift of evangelism, but he did expect us to be prepared to defend our faith. Therefore, this verse certainly seems like an example of an evangelist equipping the rest of the church for at least a modest level of evangelism.

Although the equippers mentioned in Ephesians 4:11–13 play a key role in teaching, prophecy, pastoring, evangelism, and church planting, it is clear the bulk of these ministries are to be performed by the rest of the church. However, equipping is not the end goal, nor is ministry. The end goal is spiritual maturity.

Maturing

As we discussed, the Godhead is the perfect spiritual community. And it serves as the example for the spiritual community known as the church. Jesus showed us the relationship between a Father and Son is at the heart of the community of God. We saw earlier how that relationship is reflected in the interconnected lives of spiritual parents and spiritual children in the church. Therefore, we do not need imaginary positions and titles that put one church member in charge of another. We realize bishops, presbyters, overseers, and pastors are all just different names for the same set of spiritual parents, also known as elders.

We have seen how Christ gave us apostles, prophets, evangelists, pastors, and teachers to equip the church for ministry. But we know even ministry is not the end goal because Ephesians 4:12, 13 tells us the end goal:

> So that the body of Christ may be built up until we all reach unity in the faith and in the knowledge of the Son of God and become mature, attaining to the whole measure of the fullness of Christ (NIV).

These verses are packed with meaning. But let's just highlight a few of the things that point back to the discussions we have had so far. This passage tells us the Body of Christ is built up whenever church members exercise their calling as the priesthood of all believers. They also tell us our goal should be complete unity, which we know is Christ's heartfelt desire for his church. They also talk about knowing the Son of God and attaining the whole measure of the fullness of Christ. Among other things, this speaks to the eternal life we have in a Person, not eternal life as some kind of a separate thing.

These verses also explain the end goal of equipping (which is also the end goal of all spiritual parenting): to produce fully mature disciples. But is it possible to produce fully-mature disciples within an organizational hierarchy? In order to answer that, we need to consider the original vision and clarify what it means to produce fully-mature church members.

We started our whole discussion about spiritual parents by looking at the relationship between the Father and the Son. We know Jesus had equality with God; this means he related to the Father as a mature Son, as man-to-man. We also speculated this was probably the reason why John had to prepare the way by turning the hearts of the parents to their children. Apparently, he had to prepare people for a revelation of a Parent/Child relationship that would become the pattern for spiritual parenting in the church. Now we see why.

The goal of spiritual parenting is essentially the same as natural parenting: to raise up children until they become adults—to disciple younger church members until they reach spiritual maturity. And once our spiritual children become fully mature, our relationship with them changes. No longer will we relate as parent to child, but as peer to peer.

Obviously, spiritual parents are always worthy of respect, just as natural parents are always worthy of respect. But as we all mature, we must reach a place of mutual respect, becoming equals. Jesus modeled this pattern with his own disciples in John 15:15:

> No longer do I call you servants, for the servant does
> not know what his master is doing; but I have called
> you friends, for all that I have heard from my Father
> I have made known to you.

Keep in mind that Jesus is the Messiah; he was literally their Lord. Unlike us, he would have been justified in treating his disciples like subordinates forever. Because he is the Head of the Body, he genuinely holds a superior position in the church. However, he also wanted to serve as our example.[1] Therefore, once his discipleship of the Twelve was complete, he showed us how to treat our spiritual children as they mature.

His disciples obviously learned this lesson because they followed his example.[2] Once they appointed elders in a church, they related to those elders as equals. For example, in 1 Peter 5:1, Peter did not address the elders as if he were a superior talking to subordinates; he simply appealed to the elders as "a fellow elder."[3]

However, the ultimate goal is for every church member to become fully mature in the faith. Paul emphasizes this in Colossians 1:28:

> Him we proclaim, warning everyone and teaching everyone with all wisdom, that we may present everyone mature in Christ.

We noted earlier how the writer of the book of Hebrews actually rebuked the church because the entire congregation had not yet become teachers. This means the writer expected every church member to eventually mature into a teacher—to be able to instruct others in the faith. The ultimate goal was to produce disciples capable of producing more disciples. That is the biblical picture of a fully-functioning priesthood of all believers.

---

1 **John 13:15** For I have given you an example, that you also should do just as I have done to you.

2 **1 Corinthians 11:1** Be imitators of me, as I am of Christ.

3 **1 Peter 5:1** So I exhort the elders among you, as a fellow elder …

However, today's churches tend to be organizational hierarchies. As we observed at the beginning of this book, a hierarchy is any system of persons or things ranked one above another. But the hierarchy of organizations is not just about levels; each increasing level of authority within an organization contains fewer and fewer positions at each higher level. This gives an organizational hierarchy a distinct shape: a pyramid.

Organizational hierarchy

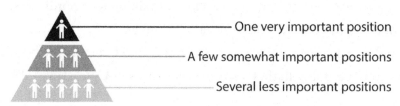

One very important position

A few somewhat important positions

Several less important positions

This organizational pyramid culminates in one very important position: the senior pastor or priest. Today, he is the only member of the church who is still expected to function in all aspects as a priest of the New Covenant. Even though the Bible tells us every member is expected to share hymns, words of instruction, revelations, and so on, most of today's congregations are content to simply sit and watch one professional church member perform all the priestly duties for the entire church.

This is not only contrary to God's vision for the church, it is contrary to the natural order he created from the beginning. As we noted earlier, the goal of natural parenting is to produce fully-mature sons and daughters, to make more adults, to eventually produce peers. This is why God's first command to Adam and Eve before the Fall was to be fruitful and multiply.[4] Their first calling was to make more people in their own image, just as God had made them in his image.

When Jesus came to restore creation, he left his disciples with a similar command: to make more disciples and to teach them everything Christ had taught his disciples; this includes his command to make more disciples.[5] Like natural parents, the disciples were expected to produce more disciples in their own image, fully mature, able to produce even more disciples. Clearly, one of the most important things Jesus taught his disciples was how to multiply themselves through discipleship.

Yet how can we follow this same pattern within an organizational hierarchy? For every position in the organized church, the person holding that position can only groom a single successor. This 1:1 ratio is the correct pattern for succession but not for multiplication. Not only that; a successor cannot assume a position until the current occupant vacates the office. This means they can never become peers.

How can a church that employs this type of organizational model ever hope to produce a true priesthood of all believers? The positions at the top of such pyramids are too limited to allow for "all believers." Instead, the organized church can only grow by increasing its base, by attracting more subordinates.

---

4   **Genesis 1:28** And God blessed them. And God said to them, "Be fruitful and multiply and fill the earth and subdue it, and have dominion over the fish of the sea and over the birds of the heavens and over every living thing that moves on the earth."

5   **Matthew 28:19, 20** Go therefore and make disciples of all nations, baptizing them in the name of the Father and of the Son and of the Holy Spirit, teaching them to observe all that I have commanded you.

Organizational growth

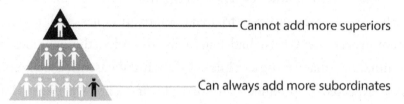

The church was never intended to become an organization, an institution, or a corporation. Although a hierarchy is an efficient model for grooming successors and directing subordinates, it is insufficient for raising spiritual sons and daughters. Such a church model is designed to produce many life-long learners but very few teachers. Or to put it another way: Sunday School is the only school from which no one ever graduates. But Christ wants us to graduate and become a true priesthood of all believers, empowered to exercise genuine spiritual authority.

Spiritual Authority

Dispelling myths about imaginary titles and positions and organizational hierarchy in the church isn't some kind of attempt to rebel against genuine spiritual authority; it's an attempt to reclaim it. Rather than appointing a single pastor to serve as our spiritual proxy, it is time we reclaimed our calling as a priesthood of all believers.

When Jesus sent out the Twelve, he gave them authority to drive out demons, cure diseases, proclaim the Gospel, and heal the sick.[1] But he never intended to limit this authority to a handful of spiritual leaders in the church; he charged his followers to make more disciples, teaching them everything he had taught them. And as we have seen throughout the preceding sections, these new disciples were expected to participate in the same ministries as the apostles and perform the same miracles. This is why Peter told the crowds in Acts 2:39:

> For the promise is for you and for your children and
> for all who are far off, everyone whom the Lord our
> God calls to himself.

Since this is true, why even have elders at all? If we all possess spiritual authority, why are we blatantly told to submit to church leaders?[2] Well, if we were uncreated and eternal like the members of the Godhead, we would all be fully mature already. But because we start as spiritual children and grow into spiritual maturity over

---

1   **Luke 9:1, 2** And he called the twelve together and gave them power and authority over all demons and to cure diseases, and he sent them out to proclaim the kingdom of God and to heal.

2   **Hebrews 13:17** Obey your leaders and submit to them, for they are keeping watch over your souls, as those who will have to give an account.

time, we need others to guide us along the way.[3] Therefore, we have elders and juniors, teachers and disciples, parents and children, not to mention the entire church community, to help guide us.

However, the church is a Body that has only one Head and that is Christ.[4] That is why elders are not supposed to lord spiritual authority over other members of the church. Biblical elders know, even though other church members are young in the faith and therefore in need of discipleship, young, immature believers are still fellow priests. This means an elder's authority is relational, not positional. Much like young Samuel needed Eli to help him recognize the voice of the Lord,[5] we need someone older and more experienced to help us discern the voice of the Lord. But the goal is for each of us to become fully mature.

Practically speaking, an elder doesn't stand between us and God and operate like our mediator. An elder assumes a spiritual posture that is more like a facilitator, helping us eventually find our own footing as fellow priests.

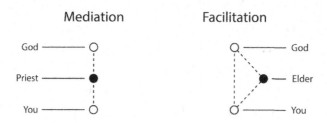

Mediation   Facilitation

God — O   O — God

Priest — ●   ● — Elder

You — O   O — You

---

3   **Deuteronomy 6:6, 7** And these words that I command you today shall be on your heart. You shall teach them diligently to your children, and shall talk of them when you sit in your house, and when you walk by the way, and when you lie down, and when you rise.

4   **Ephesians 1:22, 23** And he put all things under his feet and gave him as head over all things to the church, which is his body …

5   **1 Samuel 3:8** Then Eli perceived that the Lord was calling the boy.

Putting It All Together

Hopefully we now have a more biblical picture of the church. Although there are many details we do not know about the early church, there are many things we do know. Let's summarize them.

We know the church was originally intended to be a spiritual community based on complete unity, a reflection of the community of God. Because Christ was their sole mediator, there was no need for imaginary positions and made-up titles that placed one member above another. The early church was a genuine family, not a hierarchy. Their goal was to mutually serve one another in complete unity and to function as one Body under a single Head, which is Christ.

The Presence of Christ orchestrated their church gatherings. The Spirit prompted each member to exercise their unique spiritual gifts to build up the Body. Though some members specialized in church planting, prophecy, evangelism, pastoring, or teaching, the entire church participated in each of these ministries and more. In this way, the entire congregation learned to function as a priesthood of all believers.

The impact of this priesthood was not limited to the church. As priests, they served in helping God reconcile all things to himself. They worked to undo the curse that arose when sin was introduced into the world which caused mankind to try to subjugate and control one another. This is why the oneness of the early church became their greatest witness. When they abided in complete unity with Christ and one another, outsiders were drawn to them.

So what happens to the church's witness when we appropriate worldly ways of organizing and turn our once spiritual communities into corporations? When we take our cues from corporate America and adopt a church model that functions more like a business than a body, can we still call ourselves a church? And what does it cost us to do church this way, not just financially but spiritually? In the next part of this book, we will examine today's church model.

Part Three: Church Incorporated

"The evangelical movement has become just a bit victimized by a success-oriented culture, wanting the church—like the corporation—to be successful."

~ Henri Nouwen

Moving Backward

Hopefully, by this point, we have a clearer understanding of the early church. But how much of their example still applies to us today? How do we know whether we are merely expanding upon an early church practice or undermining it? In Acts 15, the leaders of the early church met together to discuss which Jewish traditions should rightly be observed by the Gentiles who were joining the church. After much debate, in Acts 15:10, Peter said:

> Now, therefore, why are you putting God to the test by placing a yoke on the neck of the disciples that neither our fathers nor we have been able to bear?

He was, of course, referring to the Old Covenant as recorded in the Old Testament. Later in this same passage, James summed up the heart of the matter in Acts 15:19:

> It is my judgment, therefore, that we should not make it difficult for the Gentiles who are turning to God (NIV).

The New Covenant we have through Christ is far superior to the Old Covenant.[1] Whereas even strict adherence to Old Testament Law was still insufficient, Christ's grace is more than sufficient.[2] Therefore, James rightly observed that teaching new believers to adopt the rules and regulations from the Old Covenant would only

---

1   **Hebrews 8:6** But as it is, Christ has obtained a ministry that is as much more excellent than the old as the covenant he mediates is better, since it is enacted on better promises.

2   **Galatians 2:21** I do not nullify the grace of God, for if righteousness were through the law, then Christ died for no purpose.

hinder their relationship with the Lord. So why do you suppose today's churches cannot seem to justify our current church model without drawing heavily on Old Testament, pre-church scriptures?

For example, the New Testament church did not require any kind of special building (such as a temple) because they had the revelation that the believers themselves were the real temple of God. This was a huge step forward from the way God's people worshiped him in the Old Testament. God had been longing to break out of his box and live in the midst of his people ever since the temple was first constructed.[3] Jesus predicted the glorious day when God's people would no longer worship him in a temple. He talked about it with the Samaritan woman in John 4:21–23:

> Jesus said to her, "Woman, believe me, the hour is coming when neither on this mountain nor in Jerusalem will you worship the Father. … But the hour is coming, and is now here, when the true worshipers will worship the Father in spirit and truth, for the Father is seeking such people to worship him."

As we discussed earlier, rather than buy unnecessary buildings, the early church actually sold their extra buildings in order to provide more money for the poor. Consequently, it was a huge step backward when the church eventually started buying special church buildings. Therefore, in order to rationalize today's expensive church buildings, where do we turn? Since none of the New Testament descriptions of the early church support such an idea, we have to turn to Old Testament, pre-church verses about the temple and

---

3   **Acts 7:48–50** Yet the Most High does not dwell in houses made by hands, as the prophet says, "Heaven is my throne, and the earth is my footstool. What kind of house will you build for me, says the Lord, or what is the place of my rest? Did not my hand make all these things?"

reframe them as if they are talking about today's church buildings. One such favorite is Psalm 122:1:

> I was glad when they said to me, "Let us go to the house of the Lord!"

We also know there are no New Testament verses that talk about tithing in the church. In the Old Testament, tithing was compulsory giving. And part of the tithe was used to financially support the priests. But in the New Testament church, every believer is a member of the priesthood. That would make tithing somewhat problematic since every believer would have a partial claim to the tithe. This is just one reason why giving is completely optional in the church, as explained in 2 Corinthians 9:7[4]. So, whenever we want to compel today's congregations to give tithes, where do we turn? We turn to the Old Testament and take verses like Malachi 3:8 completely out of context:

> Will man rob God? Yet you are robbing me. But you say, "How have we robbed you?" In your tithes and contributions.

Likewise, we know many New Testament churches gathered every day, not just once a week. And we know they gathered around dinner tables, not platforms. Believers ate, drank, and worshiped together. It was more like a celebration than a ceremony. Compare this to the Old Testament gathering as described in Nehemiah 8. Specifically let's look at verses 2–4, 6, 8 and 12:

---

4   **2 Corinthians 9:7** Each one must give as he has decided in his heart, not reluctantly or under compulsion, for God loves a cheerful giver.

So Ezra the priest brought the Law before the assembly ... And he read from it facing the square before the Water Gate from early morning until midday ... And Ezra the scribe stood on a wooden platform that they had made for the purpose ... And Ezra blessed the Lord, the great God, and all the people answered, "Amen, Amen," lifting up their hands. And they bowed their heads and worshiped the Lord with their faces to the ground ... They read from the book, from the Law of God, clearly, and they gave the sense, so that the people understood the reading ... And all the people went their way to eat and drink and to send portions and to make great rejoicing, because they had understood the words that were declared to them.

Does that sound familiar? Ezra and the other leaders stood on a high wooden platform (v. 4), lead the people in worship (v. 6), read from God's Word (v. 3), explained the meaning (v. 8), then dismissed the crowd around midday (v. 12) so everyone could go eat. Which description sounds more like today's church service? The New Testament party that happened around a dinner table or the Old Testament audience that gathered around a platform, listened to a lecture, then left for lunch?

This is not to say the Old Testament (or the Old Covenant) isn't incredibly valuable. On the contrary, the more we understand the Old Testament, the more we can appreciate the New Testament. But in order to do that, we must understand which things in the Old Testament were meant as a type or shadow of things to come, then apprehend the reality that can only be found on this side of the cross.[5]

It's not only Old Testament traditions that can hinder the church and inhibit our freedom in Christ. We also have to be wary of imitating the world and applying its philosophies, systems, and practices to the church. As Paul says in Colossians 2:8:

> See to it that no one takes you captive by philosophy and empty deceit, according to human tradition, according to the elemental spirits of the world, and not according to Christ.

Whenever we try to adapt the examples of the early church to our own time and culture, we must ask whether we are taking a step forward or a step backward, whether we are allowing for true freedom in Christ or restricting it. Obviously, we are not talking about imitation freedom, which is about becoming lenient toward sin.[6] That type of "freedom" only leads to death.[7] We are talking about genuine freedom, the kind that leads to life.

---

5   **Hebrews 10:1** For since the law has but a shadow of the good things to come instead of the true form of these realities, it can never, by the same sacrifices that are continually offered every year, make perfect those who draw near.

6   **Romans 6:1, 2** What shall we say then? Are we to continue in sin that grace may abound? By no means! How can we who died to sin still live in it?

7   **James 1:14, 15** But each person is tempted when he is lured and enticed by his own desire. Then desire when it has conceived gives birth to sin, and sin when it is fully grown brings forth death.

The reason why we cannot find any examples of our current church model in the New Testament is the same reason we cannot find any details about early church programs, policies, or procedures. The fact that these details are noticeably lacking is actually one of the biggest clues about the way the early church functioned.

Church Family

To claim the Bible is conspicuously silent on the way the early church functioned is like saying we cannot see the forest through the trees. The truth is actually hidden in plain sight. Clear instructions for how genuine church communities should function are written on nearly every single page of the New Testament. They are repeated over and over like the recurring theme of a symphony.

We often overlook these instructions because we come to the Scriptures with all the wrong questions. We want insights about the specific organizational structure of the early church, clues about their policies and procedures, an outline of their order-of-service, and so on. We fail to see that such questions are founded on the incorrect assumption that the early church was a religious organization, much like today's church.

In reality, the original churches were just simple Christian communities. And genuine church communities function like extended spiritual families. The reason we cannot find information about the early church's organizational structure is because the early church was not an organization. The reason there are no guidelines for running a church board meeting is because there were no church boards. This is also the reason why the requirements for church elders were only about parenting, not about running programs. Because the church was never intended to become a program.

The church was originally intended to be a spiritual family, plain and simple. And the apostles continually reiterated this vision. As Galatians 6:10 says:

> Therefore, as we have opportunity, let us do good to all people, especially to those who belong to the family of believers (NIV).

This explains why Jesus instructed his disciples to never assume titles, as told in Matthew 23:8:

> But you are not to be called rabbi, for you have one teacher, and you are all brothers.

Titles that place one disciple over another undermine our ability to treat each other like brothers. Jesus taught his disciples to function without titles—to live as a family. This is why the apostles constantly used familial language in their letters to the early churches. But it was not just sentimental; it was literal and functional. The reason we are told over and over again to view the church as our family is so we will learn to function like a family. As Paul says in 1 Timothy 5:1, 2:

> Do not rebuke an older man but encourage him as you would a father, younger men as brothers, older women as mothers, younger women as sisters, in all purity.

Our current church culture uses all the same familial language as the first believers, but our current church model is at odds with this reality. Today's churchgoers still use words like brother, sister, son, daughter, mother, and father to describe other church members. Sentimentally, we are still the same. But experientially and legally, we have become something completely different.

In order to enjoy tax breaks and protect ourselves from liability, today's churches have become corporations. Although today's churches are designated not-for-profit corporations, much like charities, they are still corporations. That makes today's churches fundamentally different from the early church communities we read about in the Bible. In order to see why, we need to understand what it means for a church to become a corporation.

Church Corporations

Although corporations were not always a dominant force in society, as they are today, the concept of the corporation is surprisingly old. The first corporations were created by the ancient Romans. In fact, our word "corporation" is derived from their Latin word *corpus*, meaning body. This is quite fitting because, in the eyes of the law, a corporation is considered an artificial person.

The legal term for such a corporate individual is *persona ficta*, meaning "fictitious person." This person is an abstraction, a legal entity that exists solely on paper as an individual "being." Though corporate "persons" are fictitious persons, they can still enjoy many of the same rights as real persons. For example, they have the right to buy and sell property, the right to enter into contracts, and the right to take someone to court.

Community	Corporation

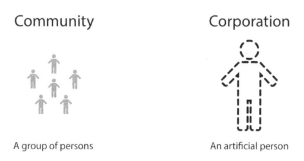

A group of persons	An artificial person

The main incentive for forming a corporation is to provide legal protection for its members; this is known as limited liability. This means, if a corporation commits a wrongdoing, the fictitious person can be held responsible while its real members may not be liable. This raises some interesting questions for the believer.

For instance, how can today's churches claim to be based on the teachings of Christ while simultaneously incorporating in order to avoid liability? How is the concept of limited liability consistent with the words of Jesus in Matthew 5:39, 40?

> But I say to you, do not resist the one who is evil. But if anyone slaps you on the right cheek, turn to him the other also. And if anyone would sue you and take your tunic, let him have your cloak as well.

I am not suggesting institutional churches should fail to legally protect themselves. In fact, it is probably a foregone conclusion for a church to incorporate once the decision has been made to institutionalize. But this does raise even deeper questions. Were churches actually meant to become institutions in the first place? Also, is there any contradiction between being a genuine church community and becoming a corporation?

Legally, a corporation is a separate person; it has its own distinct legal identity. This allows a corporation to continue to exist long after its founding members have moved on. That means, at least in theory, a corporation can exist in perpetuity, having an endless duration. Whenever a church becomes a corporation, it ensures the fictitious person can "live" forever. Basically, it is the legal form of eternal life. This probably warrants a bit more discussion, so we will touch on the idea of perpetual existence again later.

Though there are obvious advantages to becoming a corporation, we must be clear that, when we incorporate, it is the organization, not the congregation, that legally becomes the "church." In a very real sense, whenever a church community incorporates, the congregation hands over its identity to a corporation. But are we making a huge compromise by giving up our identity as the church? And if so, why does God allow it?

Counting the Cost

For the first 300 years, Christianity was more of a movement than a religion. The first believers were known for their way of life rather than a long list of religious practices. They were an informal church community that functioned much like a family. God was in their midst; the reality of his Presence and the life that poured out of his people drew unbelievers in droves.

Assuming it was God's plan for the church to continue along this trajectory, why did he eventually allow us to institutionalize the church? Why does he let us add all these imaginary titles and positions? Maybe we can find some answers in the story of Israel's kingship.

When the prophet Samuel grew old, the elders of Israel came to him saying they wanted to install a king to rule over them; they wanted to be like the other nations.[1] This made Samuel very upset but God consoled him. 1 Samuel 8:7 says:

> And the Lord said to Samuel, "Obey the voice of the people in all that they say to you, for they have not rejected you, but they have rejected me from being king over them."

Installing an earthly king was a rejection of God's kingship. However, God still allowed Israel to follow this course. In fact, after he took the crown away from Saul, God actually appointed David to be king and blessed his kingship.[2] Though the kingship itself was

---

1   **1 Samuel 8:5** Behold, you are old and your sons do not walk in your ways. Now appoint for us a king to judge us like all the nations.

2   **2 Samuel 7:16** And your house and your kingdom shall be made sure forever before me. Your throne shall be established forever.

a rejection, God still blessed David as king. Similarly, God placed Daniel under Nebuchadnezzar as ruler over Babylon.[3] And he appointed Joseph under Pharaoh as head over all of Egypt.[4] In each instance, God placed his people in positions of authority in ungodly, man-made systems.

Why? Perhaps he cares more about his people than he cares about their programs. Considering he allowed Israel to institute a kingship, why would he not allow us to institutionalize our churches? But just because God allows something does not mean he approves of it. Like Paul says in 1 Corinthians 10:23:

> "All things are lawful," but not all things are helpful.
> "All things are lawful," but not all things build up.

The question isn't whether or not we are allowed to do church this way; the question is: what does it cost us? God warned Israel that installing a king would cost them dearly. In 1 Samuel 8:10–22, he told them the king would take the best of their land, the best of their livestock, and the best of their people to serve the kingship itself.

Similarly, how much of our church budget is devoured by sheer overhead costs? How much time and energy is consumed on marketing our various church programs? How many of our people's talents are spent simply entertaining our congregations (thereby creating a low-commitment church culture)? How much time, energy, and money does our current church model require us to spend on the church itself?

---

3   **Daniel 2:48** Then the king gave Daniel high honors and many great gifts, and made him ruler over the whole province of Babylon and chief prefect over all the wise men of Babylon.

4   **Genesis 41:41** And Pharaoh said to Joseph, "See, I have set you over all the land of Egypt."

That's not to say today's churches are completely ineffective; but are they efficient? Is this truly the best way to make disciples or even a biblical way to make disciples? What is the spiritual cost of depriving most of our church members the opportunity to exercise their calling as fellow priests and to fully grow in their spiritual gifts?

Also, if installing a man as king was a rejection of God's kingship, is installing a man as the head of the church a rejection of Christ's headship? After all, why would Christ even need an organizational hierarchy to lead his church?

Command and Control

Centuries before the Romans institutionalized the church, Jesus gave his disciples a command. In Mark 10:42, 43, he said:

> And Jesus called them to him and said to them, "You know that those who are considered rulers of the Gentiles lord it over them, and their great ones exercise authority over them. But it shall not be so among you."

In that day, one particular group of Gentiles had subjugated all of Israel: the Romans. Jesus told his disciples the Gentiles did two things they should never do. They "lorded it over" others and they exercised authority over others. Though these two things are related, they are not one-and-the-same. To lord it over means "to act in a superior, domineering, or controlling manner." Obviously, Jesus did not want his disciples to adopt this attitude.

But what about the practice of exercising authority over others? As long as we maintain a humble attitude, is there anything wrong with holding a position of authority over others in the church? If Jesus was indeed condemning this practice, then his words take on a much deeper meaning. In fact, it might mean Jesus was speaking prophetically since the Romans would one day introduce positions, titles, and hierarchy into the church.

As we discussed in the beginning of this book, the very concept of one person ruling over another wasn't even considered until sin entered the world. Also, think about the revelation Paul shared about the church in Galatians 3:28:

> There is neither Jew nor Greek, there is neither slave
> nor free, there is no male and female, for you are all
> one in Christ Jesus.

It is clear that everyone in the church had equal worth in Paul's eyes. But was he also cautioning us not to hold unequal positions? Or was he cautioning us against holding positions altogether? Are the examples in this verse only about personal prejudice, or are they also about one person ruling over another? Remember, when Paul penned these words, the Gentiles ruled the Jews, slaves were subject to masters, and men dominated women.

So, what exactly is Paul getting at when he says there is no Jew, Greek, free, slave, male or female in the church? At the very least, isn't he saying there are no distinctions between members of the church? Isn't he saying there should be genuine equality in the church? If so, how does that leave room for positions, titles, and hierarchy? Do such things complement or contradict Paul's vision of the church, as described in 1 Corinthians 12:24, 25?

> But God has put the body together, giving greater
> honor to the parts that lacked it, so that there
> should be no division in the body, but that its parts
> should have equal concern for each other (NIV).

Is it even possible to have equal concern for each member when some members hold more important positions than others? After all, in a retail store, the manager is obviously more indispensable than a cashier. Likewise, in a church corporation, the senior pastor is more indispensable than an usher. If an usher suddenly had to miss church on Sunday morning, the service could go on as planned. Not so, if the senior pastor didn't show.

In any organization, a person's worth is directly connected to his position. To claim otherwise is like trying to contend a pawn is worth just as much as a king on the chessboard. Maybe that is another reason why Jesus told his disciples not to accept titles in Matthew 23:8–10:

> But you are not to be called rabbi, for you have one
> teacher, and you are all brothers. And call no man
> your father on earth, for you have one Father, who is
> in heaven. Neither be called instructors, for you have
> one instructor, the Christ.

Every organizational hierarchy culminates in a single person who holds more authority than everyone else. This model is known as the command and control (or C2) model because it allows a leader to efficiently direct the efforts of countless others under his command. That is the purpose of an organizational pyramid: to bring an entire organization under the control of a single person. The 1988 NATO definition of the command and control model is as follows:

> "Command and control is the exercise of authority
> and direction by a properly designated [individual]
> over assigned [resources] in the accomplishment of
> a [common goal]."

Even though an organization is often referred to as a "body" and its leader is known as the "head" of the organization, a human leader has limitations that prevent him from functioning like a real head. Namely, the leader of a large organization cannot communicate individually with each member in the way a real head communicates directly with each part of the body. Instead, he must work through intermediaries who can communicate his instructions to the other members.

Command and control

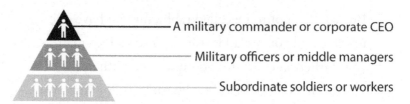

Though the word "hierarchy" did not come about until hundreds of years later, the Roman concept of authority as described in the Bible was clearly based on organizational hierarchy. While speaking to Jesus about authority, a Roman centurion actually referenced the command and control model in Matthew 8:8, 9:

> But the centurion replied, "Lord, I am not worthy
> to have you come under my roof, but only say the
> word, and my servant will be healed. For I too am
> a man under authority, with soldiers under me.
> And I say to one, 'Go,' and he goes, and to another,
> 'Come,' and he comes, and to my servant, 'Do this,'
> and he does it."

The centurion said he was a man under someone's authority with others under his own authority. He was part of a very clear military chain-of-command, a hierarchical pyramid model. Because this was the only kind of authority he knew, he used this same concept to describe Christ's spiritual authority. And, in Matthew 8:10, Jesus commended the centurion for his faith:

> When Jesus heard this, he marveled and said to
> those who followed him, "Truly, I tell you, with no
> one in Israel have I found such faith."

Even though he commended the centurion's faith, Jesus never commented on his concept of authority. This doesn't mean the centurion was wrong for saying Jesus had spiritual authority. That is beside the point. At present, we are simply discussing the filter through which the Roman centurion viewed authority—organizational hierarchy, a concept the Romans would eventually introduce to the church.

However, the Head of the church is Christ. Since he can speak directly to each member, he does not require a human hierarchy to help him lead his church. This is why he provided us with something far superior. Let's look at an example of organizational hierarchy in the Old Testament, then look at the alternative Jesus suggested.

An Old Testament Example

According to Judges 6:1, 2, the nation of Midian oppressed Israel for seven years. Midian was so powerful the Israelites had to hide in shelters in mountain clefts and caves. Therefore, Midian must have been a great military force. But long before this mighty nation became enemies of Israel, a priest of Midian named Jethro was instrumental in solving a problem for the Israelites in order to help his son-in-law, Moses.

In Exodus 18, we are told Jethro went to visit Moses while he was encamped with the rest of the Israelites in the dessert. On the second day of the visit, Moses took his seat to hear the people's disputes. This lasted from morning until evening.[1] Moses had basically become stuck being the sole mediator for the people. Partly, this was because Moses had a very special relationship with God. Exodus 33:11 tells us:

> Thus the Lord used to speak to Moses face to face, as
> a man speaks to his friend.

Ever since Moses climbed a special mountain to speak with God, everyone wanted to talk to Moses in order to discern God's mind on certain matters. However, Exodus 19:10, 11 tells us God originally wanted all the Israelites to ascend the mountain to speak with him, not just Moses.[2] God's original intention was to talk to his people face-to-face. Exodus 19:17 tells us the people got as far as the foot

---

1 **Exodus 18:13** The next day Moses sat to judge the people, and the people stood around Moses from morning till evening.

2 **Exodus 19:10, 11** The Lord said to Moses, "Go to the people and consecrate them today and tomorrow, and let them wash their garments and be ready for the third day. For on the third day the Lord will come down on Mount Sinai in the sight of all the people."

of the mountain.³ But when it came time to finally meet their God, they became afraid and devised a different plan. Exodus 20:18, 19 explains:

> Now when all the people saw the thunder and the flashes of lightning and the sound of the trumpet and the mountain smoking, the people were afraid and trembled, and they stood far off and said to Moses, "You speak to us, and we will listen; but do not let God speak to us, lest we die."

Moses tried to encourage the people to go with him to meet with God but they refused. The Israelites remained behind as Moses entered the thick cloud of smoke to meet with God.⁴ And this solidified Moses as the sole mediator between God and his people. But this burden proved too much for a single person to bear. In Exodus 18:17, 18, Jethro shared his insight about the situation:

> Moses' father-in-law said to him, "What you are doing is not good. You and the people with you will certainly wear yourselves out, for the thing is too heavy for you. You are not able to do it alone."

Then Jethro explained how Moses could implement a system that would allow him to serve as the supreme judge for all the people without having to personally interact with each and every person. He spelled out his plan in Exodus 18:21, 22:

---

3   **Exodus 19:17** Then Moses brought the people out of the camp to meet God, and they took their stand at the foot of the mountain.

4   **Exodus 20:21** The people stood far off, while Moses drew near to the thick darkness where God was.

> Moreover, look for able men from all the people, men who fear God, who are trustworthy and hate a bribe, and place such men over the people as chiefs of thousands, of hundreds, of fifties, and of tens. And let them judge the people at all times. Every great matter they shall bring to you, but any small matter they shall decide themselves. So it will be easier for you, and they will bear the burden with you.

What Jethro suggested was a system for settling disputes based on organizational hierarchy, with Moses as the pinnacle of the pyramid. It was a system of judges that functioned much like our current court system, with Moses serving as the Supreme Court. This was a truly brilliant implementation of hierarchy.

But how did Jethro come up with such a solution? The Bible doesn't tell us. All we really know about Jethro is that he was a priest of Midian. Like the Romans, the Midianites were obviously a great military force. Maybe the mindset of the Midianites was very similar to that of the Romans. Perhaps Jethro was as familiar with the command and control model as the Roman centurion. Either way, when Jesus dealt with a similar situation, he suggested a far superior solution.

A New Testament Alternative

God's longing to meet face-to-face with his people was finally fulfilled through Jesus. Because of his sacrifice on the cross, Jesus became the sole mediator for all mankind. As 1 Timothy 2:5 says:

> For there is one God, and there is one mediator
> between God and men, the man Christ Jesus …

God no longer required intermediaries to talk to us. Since this meant everyone in the church had equal access to God, they needed a different way of settling disputes than the system of judges suggested by Jethro. After all, how do you settle disputes between equals, especially when both parties believe God is on their side of the issue? Thankfully, Jesus gave us the answer. He relocated the locus of authority from the heights of a hierarchy to the midst of the community. In Matthew 18:15–17 Jesus said:

> If your brother or sister sins, go and point out their fault, just between the two of you. If they listen to you, you have won them over. But if they will not listen, take one or two others along, so that "every matter may be established by the testimony of two or three witnesses." If they still refuse to listen, tell it to the church; and if they refuse to listen even to the church, treat them as you would a pagan or a tax collector (NIV).

See how different Jesus's method is from Jethro's model? In Jethro's model, two parties first try to settle a dispute on their own. If they cannot find a resolution, they escalate the matter to the judges. If the judges cannot settle the matter, they escalate it to Moses. Jethro's process was to appeal to higher and higher levels within the hierarchy until the matter was settled.

By Jesus's method, two parties first try to settle a dispute on their own. If they cannot find a resolution, they reach out to a couple of brothers or sisters in the church to help settle the matter. If this small group cannot settle the matter, they reach out to the rest of the church. Rather than reaching upward to higher and higher levels within a hierarchy, Jesus urged us to reach outward to wider and wider circles of our community.

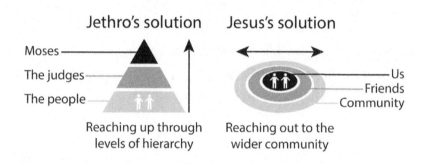

Jethro suggested instituting a hierarchy because of Moses's personal limitations; Moses simply could not handle the load all by himself. He could not personally settle every dispute, hear every complaint, or grant every request. As the people's sole mediator, he was insufficient because he was a mere mortal.

Even though God allowed Jethro's solution to be in effect for a time, it was never his long-term plan. God wanted to relate to each of us personally. He wanted to be God-with-us, to lead us one-on-one. As we noted before, Joel 2:28, 29 spoke of the day God would finally fulfill his plan:

And it shall come to pass afterward, that I will pour out my Spirit on all flesh; your sons and your daughters shall prophesy, your old men shall dream dreams, and your young men shall see visions. Even on the male and female servants in those days I will pour out my Spirit.

In Acts 2:16–21, Peter declared this prophecy was fulfilled the day the church was born. Because Jesus is the Head of the church and he is not limited like a mortal man, he can talk to each member directly, rather than relating to us through some kind of chain-of-command.

In fact, this is one reason why the church is described as a Body, because each part is controlled directly by a single Head, which is Christ.[1] Since we no longer relate to God on a second-hand basis, we can also make our requests to him directly. This is why Philippians 4:6 instructs us:

Do not be anxious about anything, but in everything by prayer and supplication with thanksgiving let your requests be made known to God.

Because the church is a priesthood of all believers with each member having equal access to God, there is no need for multiple levels of intermediaries. Whenever there is a disagreement, church members do not need to reach upward through a hierarchy to settle the matter; they only need to reach outward to their community.

But let's be clear: this is not about submitting decisions to a majority vote; it is about submitting decisions to Christ's headship.

---

1 Ephesians 4:15, 16 We are to grow up in every way into him who is the head, into Christ, from whom the whole body, joined and held together by every joint with which it is equipped …

The reason Christ instructed church members to reach out to the wider community was not to get several points of view on a matter; it was to discern Christ's single point of view on a matter. This is what Paul talked about in 1 Corinthians 1:10:

> I appeal to you, brothers, by the name of our Lord
> Jesus Christ, that all of you agree, and that there be
> no divisions among you, but that you be united in the
> same mind and the same judgment.

The reason to reach out to multiple believers is not to get multiple opinions but to get more and more confirmation of Christ's single opinion. Instead of bringing many hearts and minds to bear on every single problem, the church is to settle disputes by becoming one in heart and mind, by having complete unity. This is why Paul was so frustrated when church members in Corinth began taking one another to court. In 1 Corinthians 6:5 he said:

> I say this to shame you. Is it possible that there is
> nobody among you wise enough to judge a dispute
> between believers? (NIV).

Notice here that Paul did not tell them to take their disputes to someone in a position of authority in the church. Why not? Wouldn't that be the fastest way to settle a matter? Paul didn't suggest appealing to someone in a position of authority because there were no such positions in the early church. Christ led his church directly, as the Head of his Body. And he made his will known through the community. This is why, in the early church, there were spiritual mothers and fathers but there were no titles, offices, and positions. This also means there was no gender inequality in the early church.

Gender Inequality

There are several verses in Paul's letters that seem to promote gender inequality in the church.[1] At first glance, it seems Paul believed women are to be subordinate to men; apparently, women need to cover their heads, remain silent in church gatherings, submit to their husbands, save their questions until they get home, and not aspire to the same level of leadership as men. There has been a lot of scholarly debate about these verses, producing widely varying conclusions that run the gamut from mistranslations, misinterpretations and misogyny, to straightforward, God-ordained patriarchy.

Because the church had become an institution by the time the Bible was translated, some people believe the male-dominated

---

1 **1 Corinthians 11:3** But I want you to understand that the head of every man is Christ, the head of a wife is her husband, and the head of Christ is God.

1 Corinthians 11:7–9 For a man ought not to cover his head, since he is the image and glory of God, but woman is the glory of man. For man was not made from woman, but woman from man. Neither was man created for woman, but woman for man.

1 Corinthians 14:34, 35 The women should keep silent in the churches. For they are not permitted to speak, but should be in submission, as the Law also says. If there is anything they desire to learn, let them ask their husbands at home. For it is shameful for a woman to speak in church.

Ephesians 5:22–24 Wives, submit to your own husbands, as to the Lord. For the husband is the head of the wife even as Christ is the head of the church, his body, and is himself its Savior. Now as the church submits to Christ, so also wives should submit in everything to their husbands.

Colossians 3:18 Wives, submit to your husbands, as is fitting in the Lord.

1 Timothy 2:11–15 Let a woman learn quietly with all submissiveness. I do not permit a woman to teach or to exercise authority over a man; rather, she is to remain quiet. For Adam was formed first, then Eve; and Adam was not deceived, but the woman was deceived and became a transgressor. Yet she will be saved through childbearing—if they continue in faith and love and holiness, with self-control.

hierarchy of the organized church colored our interpretations of the original text. Others believe the text is accurately translated but the meaning is completely misinterpreted; Paul was addressing specific issues in specific churches or specific traditions in specific cultures that simply do not apply to believers in other churches, times, and cultures. Still others believe the text says what it says and means what it means; wives are subordinate to husbands and men have more spiritual authority, both at home and in the church.

Although there are a few theories that have plausible explanations for how and why Paul's true perspective on women became distorted by church tradition, such hypotheses deserve (and already have) their own books. For our discussion, we will simply look at some other scriptures that might help us unlock these more problematic passages. After all, we know many passages of Scripture simply do not make sense by themselves. Even some of Christ's own teachings make no sense when taken out of context. Consider Luke 14:26:

> If anyone comes to me and does not hate father and
> mother, wife and children, brothers and sisters—yes,
> even their own life—such a person cannot be my
> disciple (NIV).

Or consider his teaching about plucking out your eye or cutting off your hand to keep from sinning.[2] Or his teaching about eating

---

2   **Matthew 5:29, 30** If your right eye causes you to sin, tear it out and throw
    it away. For it is better that you lose one of your members than that your
    whole body be thrown into hell. And if your right hand causes you to
    sin, cut it off and throw it away. For it is better that you lose one of your
    members than that your whole body go into hell.

his flesh and drinking his blood.[3] If we did not realize these were figures of speech or metaphors, such passages would seem more than radical; they would appear downright insane. And more importantly, they would contradict the rest of Scripture. The reason we do not struggle with the real meaning of these particular passages is because we have context. We understand these verses in light of all the other things Jesus said and did.

Therefore, we need to place Paul's more controversial comments about women into the larger context of Scripture, regardless of whether or not we think they seem quite clear on their own. When we do so, the first thing we notice is many of the passages about female submission are actually part of a larger discussion on mutual submission between husbands and wives.[4] This is especially evident in verses like 1 Corinthians 7:4:

> For the wife does not have authority over her own
> body, but the husband does. Likewise the husband
> does not have authority over his own body, but the
> wife does.

---

3   **John 6:54, 56** Whoever feeds on my flesh and drinks my blood has eternal life, and I will raise him up on the last day. For my flesh is true food, and my blood is true drink. Whoever feeds on my flesh and drinks my blood abides in me, and I in him.

4   **1 Corinthians 11:11, 12** Nevertheless, in the Lord woman is not independent of man nor man of woman; for as woman was made from man, so man is now born of woman. And all things are from God.

Ephesians 5:21 Submitting to one another out of reverence for Christ.

Ephesians 5:25 Husbands, love your wives, as Christ loved the church and gave himself up for her ...

Colossians 3:19 Husbands, love your wives, and do not be harsh with them.

In addition, in each letter where Paul seems to promote the subjugation of women, he also urges slaves to be subject to their masters.[5] Thankfully, because we have already put Paul's comments about slaves into a larger context, we know Paul did not condone slavery. In 1 Timothy 1:9–11, Paul lists several types of sinners whom he considers "lawbreakers and rebels, ungodly and sinful, unholy and irreligious," including slave traders. Obviously, Paul would not include slave traders on this list unless he considered slavery itself to be a sin. Since Paul knew slavery is sinful, why did he repeatedly urge slaves to be subject to their masters? He explains his reasoning in 1 Corinthians 7:17–24:

> Nevertheless, each person should live as a believer in whatever situation the Lord has assigned to them, just as God has called them. This is the rule I lay down

---

5   **1 Corinthians 7:21** Were you a slave when you were called? Don't let it trouble you—although if you can gain your freedom, do so (NIV).

    Ephesians 6:5–8 Slaves, obey your earthly masters with respect and fear, and with sincerity of heart, just as you would obey Christ. Obey them not only to win their favor when their eye is on you, but as slaves of Christ, doing the will of God from your heart. Serve wholeheartedly, as if you were serving the Lord, not people, because you know that the Lord will reward each one for whatever good they do, whether they are slave or free (NIV).

    Colossians 3:22, 23 Slaves, obey your earthly masters in everything; and do it, not only when their eye is on you and to curry their favor, but with sincerity of heart and reverence for the Lord. Whatever you do, work at it with all your heart, as working for the Lord, not for human masters … (NIV).

    1 Timothy 6:1, 2 All who are under the yoke of slavery should consider their masters worthy of full respect, so that God's name and our teaching may not be slandered. Those who have believing masters should not show them disrespect just because they are fellow believers. Instead, they should serve them even better because their masters are dear to them as fellow believers and are devoted to the welfare of their slaves (NIV).

    Titus 2:9 Teach slaves to be subject to their masters in everything, to try to please them, not to talk back to them … (NIV).

in all the churches ... Each person should remain in the situation they were in when God called them. Were you a slave when you were called? Don't let it trouble you—although if you can gain your freedom, do so. For the one who was a slave when called to faith in the Lord is the Lord's freed person; similarly, the one who was free when called is Christ's slave. You were bought at a price; do not become slaves of human beings. Brothers and sisters, each person, as responsible to God, should remain in the situation they were in when God called them (NIV).

If we truly pay attention to what Paul said in this passage, he was not just talking about slavery but using slavery as an example for any ungodly system in which believers find themselves. This provides the much-needed context to help us interpret Paul's comments about slavery and it also sets up the discussion for gender equality.

Though Paul believed slavery was evil, his solution was to focus on saving souls, not on trying to redeem man-made systems. Though he urged slaves to procure their freedom whenever possible, his main strategy was for believing slaves to humble themselves and win over their masters through submission and obedience. Paul urged Titus to instruct slaves to employ this strategy in Titus 2:9, 10:

Teach slaves to be subject to their masters in everything, to try to please them, not to talk back to them, and not to steal from them, but to show that they can be fully trusted, so that in every way they will make the teaching about God our Savior attractive (NIV).

Paul realized, as masters and slaves were added to the kingdom, they would eventually be confronted with the reality that there is "neither slave nor free" in the church.[6] In this way, slavery would eventually crumble. But it would do so without having to politicize the Gospel or attack the system.[7]

Of course, the same verse that tells us there is "neither slave nor free" also tells us "there is no male and female" in the church. Yet we do not seem to read Paul's comments about women through the same lens as his comments about slaves. Take Colossians 3:18–24 as an example:

> Wives, submit yourselves to your husbands, as is fitting in the Lord. Husbands, love your wives and do not be harsh with them. Children, obey your parents in everything, for this pleases the Lord. Fathers, do not embitter your children, or they will become discouraged. Slaves, obey your earthly masters in everything; and do it, not only when their eye is on you and to curry their favor, but with sincerity of heart and reverence for the Lord. Whatever you do, work at it with all your heart, as working for the Lord, not for human masters, since you know that you will receive an inheritance from the Lord as a reward. It is the Lord Christ you are serving (NIV).

---

6 **Galatians 3:28** There is neither Jew nor Greek, there is neither slave nor free, there is no male and female, for you are all one in Christ Jesus.

7 **2 Corinthians 10:3, 4** For though we walk in the flesh, we are not waging war according to the flesh. For the weapons of our warfare are not of the flesh but have divine power to destroy strongholds.

After urging wives to submit to their husbands, this passage briefly talks about mutual submission within the family; it then goes into great detail about slaves submitting to their masters. It urges slaves to not only submit to their masters but to view their submission as service to the Lord, expecting a heavenly inheritance in return for their sincere submission. So how are we able to read a passage that seems to promote the subjugation of slaves even more than it does the subjugation of women, yet come away believing the subjugation of slaves is sinful and the subjugation of women is biblical?

How do we not realize it is glaringly inconsistent to pick and choose which pieces of passages we take at face value? Surely, it is because we have taken the verses that seem to subjugate slaves and placed them into a larger scriptural context, but have failed to do the same with the verses that seem to subjugate women. So what is that larger context in regard to women? We have already seen several pieces of the puzzle in previous sections of this book. Let's continue putting the picture together.

We now know *presbýteros*, the Greek word for elder, was used to describe both older men and older women. We also know Paul, who penned those disputed passages about women, worked with many women in his own ministry. (Philippians 4:2, 3 is just one example.)[8] He also commended a female *diakonos* named Phoebe, and referred to both Aquila and his wife Priscilla as his coworkers.[9]

---

8   Philippians 4:2, 3 I entreat Euodia and I entreat Syntyche to agree in the Lord. Yes, I ask you also, true companion, help these women, who have labored side by side with me in the gospel together with Clement and the rest of my fellow workers, whose names are in the book of life.

9   Romans 16:1–3 I commend to you our sister Phoebe, a deacon of the church in Cenchreae. I ask you to receive her in the Lord in a way worthy of his people and to give her any help she may need from you, for she has been the benefactor of many people, including me. Greet Priscilla and Aquila, my co-workers in Christ Jesus (NIV).

Plus, he usually mentioned Priscilla first, which probably indicated she was the more prominent minister of the two.[10] Not only that; many scholars believe Paul referenced a female apostle named Junia in Romans 16:7:

> Greet Andronicus and Junia, my fellow Jews who have been in prison with me. They are outstanding among the apostles, and they were in Christ before I was (NIV).

In light of everything above, how do we explain a verse like 1 Corinthians 14:35? Our current translations say, "For it is shameful for a woman to speak in church."[11] How did Paul affirm and work with women church leaders if he truly thought women were not even allowed to speak in the church? That makes no sense!

Clearly, he was not making a blanket statement about all women in all churches for all time. There is too much evidence from Paul's own life that contradicts this theory. But once we admit a patriarchal interpretation of such a seemingly straightforward verse as this is suspect, all such interpretations of Paul's comments about women suddenly become suspect.

A better starting point for a discussion about gender equality would be Paul's comments about the ministry of reconciliation. Paul said God's ultimate goal is to restore all things.[12] Wouldn't this

---

10 **2 Timothy 4:19** Greet Priscilla and Aquila and the household of Onesiphorus (NIV).

11 **1 Corinthians 14:35** If there is anything they desire to learn, let them ask their husbands at home. For it is shameful for a woman to speak in church.

12 **Colossians 1:19, 20** For in him all the fullness of God was pleased to dwell, and through him to reconcile to himself all things, whether on earth or in heaven, making peace by the blood of his cross.

include the way men and women were originally created to function together? Since inequality came as a result of sin, doesn't that mean God intends to restore equality?

We know God said he would one day pour out his Spirit on both men and women. And we know this scripture was fulfilled with the birth of the church. Isn't that why Paul said "there is no male and female" in the church, because gender simply does not matter when it comes to the priesthood of all believers?

If the subjugation of women was not part of God's original plan for creation, then how can it be part of his ultimate plan for the church? His ultimate plan is to create a priesthood of all believers. How is that even possible if 50% of the church is ineligible to truly function as fellow priests because of their gender? It seems somewhat paradoxical that the early church was counter-culture precisely because they embraced gender equality, yet many of today's churches are becoming counter-culture precisely because they oppose it.

Of course, much of this issue becomes a moot point once we remove man-made hierarchy from the church. After all, how can gender bias about church positions remain once we realize there are no positions in the first place? It appears the entire organizational structure of today's churches only hinders spiritual fathers and mothers from functioning as spiritual fathers and mothers. And, as we shall see, it also sends mixed signals as to who is a member of the crowd and who is a member of the congregation.

Crowds versus Congregations

Since Jesus is our example in all things, could his earthly ministry teach us something about how churches should function? Of course. But we must not confuse his private ministry with his public ministry. If we want to apply Christ's pattern of ministry to the church, we need to distinguish between ministering to our congregations and ministering to the crowds. This doesn't mean we shouldn't minister to both. But we need to approach these as two separate ministries, not one-and-the-same.

Jesus went from town to town healing the sick, performing miracles and teaching the crowds. Many of these crowds followed him.[1] He ministered to them often and had great compassion on them because they seemed "like sheep without a shepherd."[2] However, Jesus also selected twelve followers whom he designated apostles.[3] And his ministry to the Twelve was much different than his ministry to the masses. Verses like Matthew 13:10, 11 make this clear:

> Then the disciples came and said to him, "Why do you speak to them in parables?" And he answered them, "To you it has been given to know the secrets of the kingdom of heaven, but to them it has not been given."

---

1   **Matthew 4:25** And great crowds followed him from Galilee and the Decapolis, and from Jerusalem and Judea, and from beyond the Jordan.

2   **Mark 6:34** When he went ashore he saw a great crowd, and he had compassion on them, because they were like sheep without a shepherd. And he began to teach them many things.

3   **Luke 6:12, 13** In these days he went out to the mountain to pray, and all night he continued in prayer to God. And when day came, he called his disciples and chose from them twelve, whom he named apostles ...

Though Jesus ministered to everyone, he did not make disciples of everyone. Though he preached to, performed miracles for, and healed the crowds, he did not commission the crowds to preach, perform miracles, and heal others. He only taught his disciples to do such things.[4] Clearly, he had two separate ministries: those he simply ministered to and those he taught to minister. If his approach provides a pattern for the church, we could probably interpret his example in one of two ways.

On the one hand, Jesus's example of ministry to the crowds may be perceived as the forerunner to today's organized churches. In this interpretation, Jesus is the example of today's senior pastor, the disciples are the pastor's church staff, and the crowds are his congregation. Because the crowds that followed Jesus were very large, this type of ministry could be seen as the predecessor to the megachurch.

On the other hand, Jesus's example may be perceived as the pattern for the small, house churches we read about in the New Testament. In this interpretation, Jesus functions as the Head, the disciples function as his Body (meaning the church itself) and the crowds are the mission field. Because the crowds that followed Jesus were massive, this type of ministry could serve as an example of the huge impact that can be made by just one small church.

The first interpretation is a very inward-focused group; the church is a large congregation in which most of its members are passive recipients and the staff performs all the real ministry. The second interpretation is a very outward-focused group; the church is a small congregation that has a big impact on all the people around it because every member participates in the ministry.

---

4   **John 4:2** Although Jesus himself did not baptize, but only his disciples …

Matthew 10:8 Heal the sick, raise the dead, cleanse lepers, cast out demons.

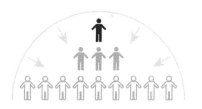

A megachurch ministering inward   A housechurch ministering outward

🧍 = Jesus   🧍 = Disciples   🧍 = Crowds

Either way, we know Jesus made his ministry to the Twelve his main priority. The disciples had more access to Jesus than the crowds and often spent time with him privately, away from the crowds.[5] When it came to discipleship, Jesus clearly chose to invest a large amount of time into a small number of people, rather than a small amount of time into a large number of people.

Just because Jesus poured more of himself into his disciples than he did the multitudes, we shouldn't think he wasn't trying to reach

---

5   **Matthew 17:19** Then the disciples came to Jesus privately …

    Matthew 24:3 As he sat on the Mount of Olives, the disciples came to him privately …

    Luke 10:23 Then turning to the disciples he said privately …

    Mark 6:31 And he said to them, "Come away by yourselves to a desolate place and rest a while."

    Luke 9:18 Now it happened that as he was praying alone, the disciples were with him.

    John 18:1, 2 When Jesus had spoken these words, he went out with his disciples across the brook Kidron, where there was a garden, which he and his disciples entered. Now Judas, who betrayed him, also knew the place, for Jesus often met there with his disciples.

the multitudes. If Jesus had run after the crowds and spread himself too thin, he might have produced more disciples on the front end, but would not have produced many mature disciples in the long run. And only mature disciples can make more disciples. Adequate teachers produce good students. Excellent teachers produce more teachers. To truly follow Jesus's pattern, we cannot simply build a big roof over a crowd and call them a congregation.

The Jesus Store

A common rationale for big church buildings is that today's congregations are simply too large to meet in ordinary homes. However, the moment we erect a church building, we also put up a church sign. But why do we do this? Is it so our fellow church members can easily find the building? Obviously, our congregation already knows the location. Signage is used to increase public recognition and buy-in. Therefore, the main purpose of a church sign is to attract outsiders. And this is known as marketing.

Similarly, church greeters, outreach programs, welcome centers, and new member orientation classes are all designed to attract and retain outsiders. Obviously, our big church buildings are not just larger venues for our existing members; they also serve as storefronts to attract new ones.

But if a genuine church community is supposed to function like a family, is a storefront the best strategy for growing a spiritual family? After all, how do natural families grow? They can grow in one of three ways: through marriage, birth, or adoption.

Each entryway into a natural family is through one of three relationships that includes its own unique experience. If you are married, you know what it means to be one with your spouse. If you were raised by your biological parents, you probably grew up hearing how much you resemble your mom or your dad. If you were adopted, you should know how special it is to be specifically chosen.

Originally, people entered the spiritual family of the church through these same three avenues of relationship. As previously discussed, the church is the Bride of Christ. Therefore, all believers know what it means to be married into the family of God. Likewise, we are born into the family of God[1] and we are adopted into the family of God.[2] Through the church, we experience all three ways of belonging to God. We are one with God, we are formed in his image, and we are specifically chosen: married, born, and adopted.

Marriage	Birth	Adoption
is about being one	is about being alike	is about being chosen

But creating a storefront provides another avenue into the church that can circumvent all of these relationships. By setting up shop and hanging out a shingle, we invite walk-ins, with or without relationship. That's not to say relationship isn't part of the overall plan. It is most certainly the goal to invite outsiders into the church, present them with the Gospel, and usher them into a real relationship with God and other members of the church. However, the storefront model also makes it easy for some members to simply fall through the cracks. Since new members can easily enter without preexisting relationships to other members, they can just as easily leave unnoticed.

---

1 **John 5:1** Everyone who believes that Jesus is the Christ has been born of God, and everyone who loves the Father loves whoever has been born of him.

2 **Ephesians 1:4, 5** In love he predestined us for adoption …

Furthermore, this model blurs the line between membership and discipleship. And that has consequences. Whereas mere membership is only transactional, discipleship must be relational. But when we employ a storefront model of ministry, members of the crowd might easily mistake themselves for members of the congregation, simply because they attend services and donate money.

In our efforts to remove the barriers to entry, have we lowered the bar instead? Whereas a storefront is completely customer-focused, a genuine church community is supposed to be wholly Christ-focused. Yet organizational membership doesn't even come close to the cost of true discipleship. Consider what Jesus said in Luke 14:33:

> So therefore, any one of you who does not renounce
> all that he has cannot be my disciple.

Also, the storefront model is limited by the size of the physical church building. In order to preach the Gospel to a hundred people, we need a sanctuary that seats a hundred people; in order to preach the Gospel to a thousand people, we need a sanctuary that seats a thousand people, and so on. This is the hard cost of employing a ministry model that relies on drawing crowds to our own doorstep rather than taking the Gospel to theirs, as Jesus commanded.[3]

And this model not only incentivizes us to increase the size of our church facilities, but to increase the number of church amenities as well. Many of today's churches have comfortable seating, air-conditioning, professional sound and video equipment, free coffee, parking lot shuttles, and more. Not to mention all the elaborate music and drama productions, outdoor concerts, and kids' carnivals.

---

3   **Matthew 28:19** Go therefore and make disciples of all nations ...

Even though such efforts are successful at attracting some people, they are equally successful at repelling others. One big criticism many non-churchgoers level at today's churches is the exorbitant amount of money congregations seem to spend on themselves instead of investing in something more worthwhile, such as helping the poor.

The Least of These

Though many churches spend a lot of money on themselves, their intentions are not necessarily selfish. Some churches sincerely believe they need to have the best carpeting, furniture, decor, equipment, and vehicles money can buy. And they try to put on the best programs and performances they can afford. Why? Because constructing a church building, buying all the furnishings, equipment and resources for it, as well as funding all the programs and events that go along with it, are all performed as acts of worship.

Do some of these expenses seem extravagant? Perhaps. But worship is supposed to be extravagant, especially when we are honoring the God of all creation.[1] Could these same resources be spent elsewhere, such as helping the poor? Absolutely. But unless a church attracts enough members, how can it generate enough resources to help the poor? Therefore, even churches that add seemingly superfluous attractions like bookstores, coffee shops, and gymnasiums often do so in order to attract more members to help serve the greater good. Plus, as long as all this extravagance lavishes love upon the Lord, how can it be wrong?

Maybe the story of the woman who anointed Jesus can give us some insight. After all, this is probably the most famous story of extravagant worship in the New Testament. John 12 tells the story of a woman who anointed Jesus with a very expensive jar of perfume shortly before his death. After anointing him, Judas rebuked her, saying she should have sold the perfume and given the money to the poor. Though that sounded noble, Jesus actually defended the woman in John 12:7, 8:

---

1 **Revelation 4:11** Worthy are you, our Lord and God, to receive glory and honor and power, for you created all things, and by your will they existed and were created.

Jesus said, "Leave her alone, so that she may keep it for the day of my burial. For the poor you always have with you, but you do not always have me."

Jesus condoned this woman's seemingly wasteful act of worship. And why not? For one thing, whether she realized it or not, she was preparing him for his burial. For another, he was only going to be here in the flesh for a very short time. This was her one-and-only opportunity to give something tangible and extravagant to her Lord.

Even though Jesus is no longer here in the flesh, we still try to imitate this woman's extravagant act of worship in material ways. This is why we faithfully give financial support to church building projects, programs, ministries and outreach events, even if some of them seem somewhat wasteful.

But have we ever considered what made this woman's act of worship so commendable? Could it be that she gave away her most prized possession without reaping any material benefit for herself? If so, then it is hard to compare her completely selfless act of worship with all the time, money, and energy we invest in our own church buildings and church events since we get to inhabit the buildings we construct and attend the events we create. This doesn't mean our intentions are not pure, but it still sends a mixed message.

The apostle Paul was especially careful not to send such mixed messages with his own ministry. Even though he endorsed financial support for ministers of the Gospel, he often refused to personally take any payment so that no one could misinterpret his motives.[2]

---

2   **1 Corinthians 9:11, 12** If we have sown spiritual things among you, is it too much if we reap material things from you? If others share this rightful claim on you, do not we even more? Nevertheless, we have not made use of this right, but we endure anything rather than put an obstacle in the way of the gospel of Christ.

It was precisely because of his refusal to profit from his preaching that he was able to speak with so much authority, as he explained in 2 Corinthians 2:17:

> Unlike so many, we do not peddle the word of God for profit. On the contrary, in Christ we speak before God with sincerity, as those sent from God (NIV).

Perhaps this is why it seems so incongruous to outsiders whenever we buy expensive church buildings. As we discussed before, the early church sold their excess property and buildings in order to raise money for the poor. That's because the poor were a very high priority in the early church. As James 1:27 says:

> Religion that God our Father accepts as pure and faultless is this: to look after orphans and widows in their distress and to keep oneself from being polluted by the world.

Even if our main reason for buying a big church building is to attract more people who will in turn give more money to the poor, it seems a very circuitous route. Such a church model seems to resemble to an over-engineered machine—something overly complex to perform a simple task. How much money do we have to spend on sheer overhead before we can perform any real ministry? Is this really the best way to extravagantly worship the Lord?

Yes, Jesus defended the woman for using her jar of perfume to anoint him rather than selling it and giving the money to the poor. But when he left instructions for the rest of us, he never suggested we should choose between ministering to him or ministering to the poor. In fact, it was quite the opposite. In Matthew 25:31–40 he said:

When the Son of Man comes in his glory, and all the angels with him, he will sit on his glorious throne. All the nations will be gathered before him, and he will separate the people one from another as a shepherd separates the sheep from the goats. He will put the sheep on his right and the goats on his left.

Then the King will say to those on his right, "Come, you who are blessed by my Father; take your inheritance, the kingdom prepared for you since the creation of the world. For I was hungry and you gave me something to eat, I was thirsty and you gave me something to drink, I was a stranger and you invited me in, I needed clothes and you clothed me, I was sick and you looked after me, I was in prison and you came to visit me."

Then the righteous will answer him, "Lord, when did we see you hungry and feed you, or thirsty and give you something to drink? When did we see you a stranger and invite you in, or needing clothes and clothe you? When did we see you sick or in prison and go to visit you?"

The King will reply, "Truly I tell you, whatever you did for one of the least of these brothers and sisters of mine, you did for me."

Now that Jesus is no longer here in the flesh, we will never be faced with a choice between ministering to the poor or ministering to Christ because *ministering to the poor is ministering to Christ!*

This is truly profound. Jesus told us we encounter him in the flesh whenever we encounter the poor. And however we treat the poor is how we treat the Lord.

Therefore, if our churches want to become truly extravagant in the way we minister to Jesus, we simply need to become extravagant in the way we minister to the poor. Perhaps this means doing something really outrageous such as selling our church buildings and giving the money to people in need. Not only would we be following in the footsteps of the early church, but we would be forced to start thinking about church outside the box.

Raising Veal

It was the Romans who eventually institutionalized the church, starting in the early 300's. Previously, believers had only known church gatherings where each person participated in the meetings, where everyone was encouraged to bring a hymn, or a teaching, or a personal revelation, and so on. Clearly, the Romans had a very different vision for the church. And the moment Rome embraced Christianity as its national religion, they began implementing that vision.

The Romans had a great respect for oratory, the art of public speaking. This is why the layout of the new Roman church buildings made it clear the congregation was now an audience, expected to listen to lectures. One of the first things the Romans did to institutionalize the church was hire eloquent orators to serve as church priests. Employing such skilled, professional speakers helped elevate the role of priests far above their fellow church members.

Further levels of separation between these professional priests and their congregations were introduced through the addition of official robes and rituals. Over time, unbiblical words like "clergy" and "laity" entered the vocabulary of the church and solidified the divide. Likewise, special requirements for ordination were introduced and seminaries were formed. Eventually, any vision for church gatherings where every member exercised his or her calling as a fellow priest was lost and forgotten.

Many of today's churches have maintained this trajectory and fully embraced a model in which church members get spiritually fed without ever exercising their calling as fellow priests. But how long can church members be spiritually spoon-fed before they develop a dependency? Developing this kind of dependency is known as becoming institutionalized. In the movie *The Shawshank Redemption*, an inmate named Red explains how, over time, prisoners become institutionalized:

> "These walls are funny. First you hate 'em, then you get used to 'em. Enough time passes, you get so you depend on them. That's institutionalized."

Today's churchgoers enjoy sermons with PowerPoint slides, Sunday School lessons on whiteboards, Children's Church, Bible studies, book studies, podcasts, and more. But what good is all this spiritual education unless it results in genuine spiritual formation? The Body of Christ doesn't simply need to eat; it needs to exercise.

1 Corinthians 14:26 tells us we build up the Body of Christ whenever we allow each member to participate in the meetings by instructing others or by bringing hymns or sharing personal revelations, etc..[1] This is a completely different picture of church from passively listening to lectures from a handful of professional Christians.

So, what happens to a church when most of its members get spiritually fed without having the opportunity to exercise their true calling? Rather than shepherding sheep, this sounds more like raising veal.

If you are unfamiliar with the process, it looks something like this: a young calf is placed in a box. The purpose of the box is to keep the calf immobile, never allowing it to build up muscle. This ensures the calf will eventually make for tender, tasty veal. From then on,

---

1   **1 Corinthians 14:26** What then shall we say, brothers and sisters? When you come together, each of you has a hymn, or a word of instruction, a revelation, a tongue or an interpretation. Everything must be done so that the church may be built up (NIV).

the calf is constantly fed but never allowed to exercise. Over time, it grows fat and weak. Eventually, it won't even be able to survive outside its box.

A young calf is taken
from its mother

Then placed in a crate
to prevent movement

Where it is fed but not
allowed to exercise

Causing it to grow
fat and weak

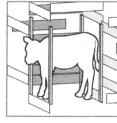

So that if the crate
is ever removed

The fattened calf
cannot survive

Much like the veal calf, many of today's churchgoers spend their entire spiritual lives inside of church boxes, both literally and figuratively. This might be the best way to develop strong institutions, but is it the best way to develop strong individuals? In our pursuit of numerical growth, are we sacrificing spiritual growth? In such a consumer-focused culture, maybe we need to be reminded of how Jesus measured the success of his own ministry.

Measuring Success

Maybe the reason we do not recognize the true cost of today's church model is because when we turn the church into an organization, we start to think like an organization—we begin measuring success in worldly terms, not spiritual terms. The standard of success becomes the size of our church budget, the scale of our next building project, and the number of people in the pews. However, Jesus used a completely different standard for measuring his own success.

At the height of his popularity when he walked the earth, Jesus had a following that would make even today's megachurch pastors envious. But due to his controversial teaching, many disciples eventually deserted him.[1] However, as Jesus was praying to the Father right before his death, he made a couple of truly mind-blowing statements about his own ministry. In John 17:4 he said:

> I have brought you glory on earth by finishing the work you gave me to do (NIV).

This means Jesus knew he was successful in his mission, despite popular opinion. So, how did he measure his success? He told us plainly in John 17:12:

> None has been lost except the one doomed to destruction so that scripture would be fulfilled (NIV).

Except for Judas who was destined to betray him, Jesus claimed, "none has been lost." Think about this for a moment. Jesus lost many disciples, possibly thousands. In terms of profits and losses, Jesus was clearly in the red. So how could he claim, "none has been lost?"

---

1   John 6:66 From this time many of his disciples turned back and no longer followed him.

Apparently, he did not consider himself responsible for the crowds; he only considered himself responsible for the Twelve. Though he ministered to everyone, the Twelve were specifically given to him by God. He even said as much in John 17:6:

> I have revealed you to those whom you gave me out
> of the world. They were yours; you gave them to me
> and they have obeyed your word (NIV).

Earlier, we discussed how Jesus made it his main priority to invest in his disciples. And now we see that he actually evaluated his entire success on how well he completed this single task.

This raises an interesting question: since Jesus is our example in all things, is this the same pattern we are supposed to follow? Is it possible God will judge the success of our ministries, not by impressive *numbers*, but by specific *names*? Does he entrust us with certain people and, even though we might minister to others, are those specific people our primary mission on this planet?

If so, what does it mean if we pursue the crowds at the expense of those with whom we were entrusted? We know the Good Shepherd is willing to leave the ninety-nine to go after the one.[2] But what happens if we leave one behind in our quest to gain ninety-nine more? Is it possible we might stand before God one day, boasting about our big ministries, saying "Lord, look at all these people I brought you," only to have him reply, "That's great. But what happened to the ones I *gave* you?"

---

2 **Matthew 18:12–14** What do you think? If a man has a hundred sheep, and one of them has gone astray, does he not leave the ninety-nine on the mountains and go in search of the one that went astray? And if he finds it, truly, I say to you, he rejoices over it more than over the ninety-nine that never went astray. So it is not the will of my Father who is in heaven that one of these little ones should perish.

Identity Theft

We know the Romans institutionalized the church and gave us the concept of the corporation. However, the first corporations were not considered artificial persons. The Romans eventually created this concept as well, but it happened hundreds of years later when its invention would be credited to Sinibaldo Fieschi, better known as Pope Innocent IV.

Before his elevation to the papacy, Sinibaldo was an expert and teacher of canon law, which was the set of laws and regulations that governed the institutional church. He even served one of the previous Popes as a canon lawyer and member of the Roman Curia. Among his more notable achievements, Pope Innocent IV authorized the use of torture for eliciting confessions from heretics. However, his most lasting legacy was the creation of the *persona ficta* or fictitious person, the legal personality ascribed to corporations. This concept was a masterful creation that helped the Pope circumvent an overt contradiction in the institutional church.

In order to support their infrastructure, monasteries needed to engage in commerce. However, many monastic orders took vows of poverty that prevented the monks from engaging in such activities. This was quite a quandary. The monks needed to make money without breaking their vow of poverty.

Drawing upon his experience as a church lawyer, the Pope created a religious loophole for the monks. He instituted a new doctrine that declared monasteries had corporate personalities that were to be considered separate, legal persons. Since the monastery was the "person" that engaged in vile commerce, its individual members could not be guilty of committing an actual sin. And since a corporate person does not have an actual soul, the corporation could not be guilty of committing a sin either. Thanks to Pope Innocent IV, the monks became free to make money and we inherited his pattern for creating soulless corporations.

As we noted earlier, corporations are fictitious persons that exist in perpetuity, meaning they have a legal form of eternal life. And we also established that it is the corporation, not the congregation, that legally becomes the church when a church community incorporates itself. Pope Innocent IV's ingenious bit of legal and doctrinal sidestepping seemed to alleviate one spiritual contradiction in the church, but did it create another?

Genesis 25 tells the story of two brothers, Esau and Jacob. Esau was the older brother and his father's favorite. This means Esau stood to gain the best inheritance; it was his birthright. However, Jacob tricked him into selling his birthright for a measly bowl of stew; Esau did not value his birthright. That is why Hebrews 12:16 warns us not to be:

> Unholy like Esau, who sold his birthright for a
> single meal.

Similarly, Eve was deceived into eating the forbidden fruit by believing the lie that it would make her "like God."[1] She failed to recall that she and Adam had been made in the image of God; they were already like him. In a sense, Esau and Eve were both victims of identity theft. Not understanding and not valuing their identities is what eventually cost them their identities.

Consequently, what does it cost when the church doesn't value her own identity? When our identity as the church is unthinkingly

---

1   **Genesis 3:4, 5** But the serpent said to the woman, "You will not surely die. For God knows that when you eat of it your eyes will be opened, and you will be like God, knowing good and evil."

handed over to a corporation in order to gain limited liability, are we despising our birthright? After all, the church was never called to pursue a legal form of eternal life for itself; it was called to extend the invitation of genuine eternal life to others. Nor is the church called to *incorporate* itself into a fictitious person; it is called to *incarnate* a real person, Jesus Christ.

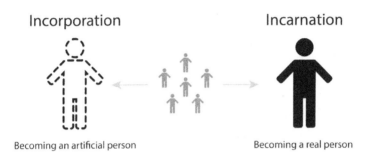

Incorporation   Incarnation

Becoming an artificial person   Becoming a real person

Part Four: Church Outside the Box

"What should young people do with their lives today? Many things, obviously. But the most daring thing is to create stable communities in which the terrible disease of loneliness can be cured."

~ Kurt Vonnegut

Pursuing Community

In his landmark book *Bowling Alone: The Collapse and Revival of American Community*, author Robert D. Putnam discusses the decline of social capital and civic engagement in America since the 1950's. Social capital is the collective value of social networks, a gauge for measuring the health of a society. One reason he cites for the decline in social capital is the migration from small town living to life in the suburbs. Once the automobile became ubiquitous in America, city planners quit planning small communities and began zoning entire cities around commuters.

Some areas of the city became residential districts, others became industrial, others became shopping districts, and so on. For many of us today, there is no option to walk to the corner grocer because there are no corner grocers. We drive to the shopping center, drive to work, and drive our kids to school. And each destination is in a different part of town. Plus, most of our friends now live in other neighborhoods.

This way of living makes us better consumers, but not very good neighbors. Instead of walking next door to the neighbor's house to borrow a cup of sugar, we have to hop in the car and drive to Walmart because we no longer know our neighbors. We do not live in community by default anymore. That means most Americans simply do not live any kind of shared community life.

This undermines one of the basic behaviors of healthy communities: mutual reciprocity. In a healthy community, people don't assist one another on a merely transactional basis. Meaning, I don't do a favor for you expecting payment from you in return. I simply do it because you are my neighbor, a member of my community. And I have the assurance others in the community will do the same for me. Even though you might not be the one returning the favor, I still benefit from helping you because living in this type of community benefits me. We don't need to bother with a one-to-one exchange of favors or worry about keeping score. Eventually, everyone will be rewarded for contributing to the community.

As an example, take a community barn-raising. Once upon a time, barn-raisings were a common occurrence across rural North America. Barns were used to store hay and animals; this made them a necessity for every farmer. However, they were incredibly costly to build because of the sheer labor required to raise a barn. But for farmers who lived in community with other farmers, this was no problem. Neighbors simply helped build barns for one another, eliminating the labor costs. Each member of the community willingly turned out to help because each person knew the favor would eventually be returned.

Similarly, the early churches were genuine communities. Believers didn't just come together once or twice a week to exchange stories about their separate spiritual lives; they lived a shared spiritual life. This means they bore each other's burdens—one of the main ingredients of true spiritual community.

Having community with other believers means more than simply having similar beliefs; it means ordering your day-to-day lives around one another. The more interdependence among the members of a group, the more spiritual community they will have. That is why creating genuine church community often starts with proximity. The closer believers live to one another, the more day-to-day life they can share with each other.

Naturally, the example of early church community is easier to duplicate in some places than others. There are still plenty of small towns in America where everyone knows their neighbors, where they all shop at the same corner store, and all their kids attend the same little, country school. This may not be the same level of interdependence as the early churches but it is a good starting point. Every member in a small town already has a certain degree of community by default. In other places, creating genuine community is more challenging. It takes concerted effort and real sacrifice. However, it is well worth it.

In the documentary *Happy*, filmmaker Roko Belic explores the subject of human happiness through interviews with people all over the world, from several walks of life. The lofty goal of this documentary is to find out what actually makes people happy. One huge takeaway from the film is the realization that people are created for community. Out of all the countries examined, the filmmaker concludes the happiest place on the planet is Denmark. There are several reasons for this, but the most significant factor is community.

Out of all the industrialized nations, Denmark has more of its population living in co-housing communities than any other country. What is a co-housing community? Just what it sounds like. Multiple families live in the same building with separate apartments for each family and common areas for group meals and other gatherings. Families take turns cooking meals, doing chores, and watching kids. The families are truly interdependent. The distribution of labor and sharing of resources makes life much less burdensome than if everyone lived in separate homes and had to survive solely on their own incomes.

That's not to say non-institutional Christians are required to move into communes. But if you are truly looking to apprehend what it means to become a genuine church community, it's not enough to simply leave behind the institutional church model; you must become intentional about creating some kind of authentic community with other believers. You must find ways to integrate yourself into a spiritual family, to intertwine your life with the lives of other church members. You must go beyond merely hearing each other's problems; you must start bearing each other's burdens. Obviously, this can take many forms.

In our church community for example, there are families who share homes with other families, and families that have moved into the same apartment complex or neighborhood. There are also members who have intentionally taken jobs at the same company. Whatever it takes to create as much overlap as possible. This often requires real sacrifice: changing living arrangements and career plans just to become more connected with other members of the church. Some families have even moved from other states just to become part of our community.

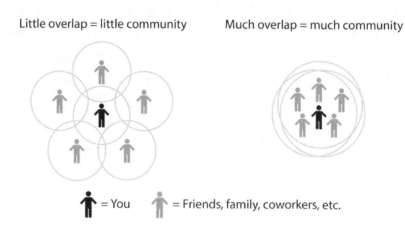

Little overlap = little community   Much overlap = much community

= You   = Friends, family, coworkers, etc.

Other believers in other communities do things a bit differently. For instance, multiple families might buy a building and renovate it, creating separate apartments for each family, along with a shared common area for group meals. This is basically the Danish co-housing approach applied to urban America. Still others move into planned neighborhoods with community buildings and playgrounds in the middle of the neighborhood for group meals, recreation, and more. It is very similar to co-housing but with a bit more personal space. And some even move into old-fashioned communes.

Whatever form it takes, it is all about moving from independence to interdependence, from being just a group of individuals to becoming a single body of believers. Not to mention what a witness it is for unbelievers to see a church taking care of actual people's needs rather than re-carpeting an old sanctuary or raising money for a new one.

Also, it is very fulfilling to have a complete church experience rather than a compartmentalized one. Instead of driving across town once or twice a week to fellowship in a special building, you get to live a shared spiritual life every day, in your own homes. Instead of church being an event that happens at a dedicated time in a dedicated place, it becomes a way of life that happens all the time, in every place. Instead of being just a commuter, you get to be part of a genuine community.

Experiencing Worship

One concern believers have about leaving the institutional church is giving up a great corporate worship experience. They worry that a small house church gathering cannot compete with a Sunday morning service. That concern is not unfounded. However, it is a very incomplete picture of corporate worship.

This might be a bit of an oversimplification but there seem to be two opposite ends to the corporate worship spectrum. And each of these two types of worship has its own merits. On one end of the spectrum is the loud music and blowout spectacle associated with non-denominational and charismatic churches. These are the churches with a full band, giant speakers, and stage lights. On the other end of the spectrum is the contemplative silence and powerful symbolism of high church worship. These are the churches with robes, rituals, and candles. Even though we associate many of these worship experiences with church buildings, they are not confined to church buildings.

If you have attended enough Christian concerts and worship events, you know God can be powerfully present outside the church walls. In fact, many non-denominational and charismatic churches are basically putting on a worship concert every week. It just happens to be the same band in the same building every Sunday. But at an actual worship concert, the crowd is sometimes even more engaged because they know and like all the songs being performed. And if God shows up and starts moving, there is no pressure to cut him off due to a tight Sunday morning schedule. Not to mention the money from the ticket sales can support the artists and hopefully create more amazing worship events.

Likewise, many believers who have gone on short-term mission trips or retreats have often partaken of communion, practiced prayer vigils, and had many other high church worship experiences outside the church walls. They can attest these types of practices transfer quite easily to non-institutional settings because they do not depend on any kind of special lighting or sound equipment or anything else that ties them to a particular venue.

Granted, you might have less opportunity to participate in either of these types of worship experiences outside an institutional church setting. But as long as you remain in the institutional church, you are probably being deprived of one of the most important forms of worship practiced by the early church. This is because it works best in smaller, informal settings. I am talking about the Lord's Supper, the way it was meant to be experienced. 1 Corinthians 11:23–26 tells us:

> The Lord Jesus on the night when he was betrayed took bread, and when he had given thanks, he broke it, and said, "This is my body which is for you. Do this in remembrance of me." In the same way also he took the cup, after supper, saying, "This cup is the new covenant in my blood. Do this, as often as you drink it, in remembrance of me." For as often as you eat this bread and drink the cup, you proclaim the Lord's death until he comes.

The Lord's Supper can be a powerful act of worship because it can turn every meal into a remembrance of Christ's sacrifice. For the early church, these meals soon became full-on celebrations known as "love feasts."[1] Apparently the love feasts turned into such a party, Paul actually had to reign in the early church because some members were getting drunk and causing problems.[2]

In today's church gatherings, the Lord's Supper is often reduced to an aspirin-sized piece of bread and a shot glass full of juice. It's easier to serve large numbers of people this way. But we also end up reducing an all-night celebration to a single moment of communion and we remove every semblance of "supper" from the Lord's Supper. Rather than enjoying a full-on feast with our church family, we look like we're merely taking medication.

I am not mocking the Lord's Supper; if anything, I want to see the church recover it. How amazing is it to realize there is a legitimate form of worship that looks like a house party? But it makes sense. What better way to express the life of Christ than through a raucous, rambunctious family feast? So yes, the worship experiences you have in genuine church community may look a lot different from the high energy Christian concerts and high church rituals. But they can certainly express just as much life. Maybe even more.

---

1   **Jude 12** These are hidden reefs at your love feasts ...

2   **1 Corinthians 11:20, 21** For in eating, each one goes ahead with his own meal. One goes hungry, another gets drunk.

Receiving Power

In most institutional churches, only a handful of people get to continually operate in their calling and exercise their spiritual gifts. It's not intentional; it's logistical. In small gatherings, everyone can participate. In large gatherings, the leaders must function as proxies for the priesthood of all believers. This lack of participation by the entire congregation often lowers our expectations of ourselves. Our full-time church leaders tend to look spiritually superior by comparison because our current church model hinders the spiritual growth of most other church members.

Of course, that is a sweeping generalization. Many church leaders are truly amazing by any standard. But so are you, or at least you could be. Sadly, you may never realize it without more opportunities to exercise your spiritual gifts. Finding a church community where you can finally reclaim your calling as a fellow priest can be absolutely life-changing. In fact, it might even redefine your expectations of the average Christian. Just look at Jesus's expectations for the average believer in John 14:12:

> Truly, truly, I say to you, whoever believes in me will also do the works that I do; and greater works than these will he do, because I am going to the Father.

For anyone who thinks Jesus was only talking about the apostles, Paul makes it clear every single believer is expected to do extraordinary things. Just look at what he says about spiritual gifts in 1 Corinthians 12:7–11:

> *To each* is given the manifestation of the Spirit for the common good. For to one is given through the Spirit the utterance of wisdom, and to another the

utterance of knowledge according to the same Spirit, to another faith by the same Spirit, to another gifts of healing by the one Spirit, to another the working of miracles, to another prophecy, to another the ability to distinguish between spirits, to another various kinds of tongues, to another the interpretation of tongues. All these are empowered by one and the same Spirit, who apportions *to each one* individually as he wills. (Italics added.)

Twice in this passage, Paul emphasizes the fact that God gives spiritual gifts to each member of the church. Similarly, consider Stephen and Philip. Their main responsibility was to run what we might think of as the first church food pantry.[1] But they looked like Christian superstars by today's standards. Consider what Acts 6:8 says about Stephen:

And Stephen, full of grace and power, was doing great wonders and signs among the people.

And read what Acts 8:6 says about Philip:

And the crowds with one accord paid attention to what was being said by Philip when they heard him and saw the signs that he did.

So why did such a blatantly supernatural community downshift into such a non-supernatural way of doing things? Personally, I

---

1   Acts 6:5 And what they said pleased the whole gathering, and they chose Stephen, a man full of faith and of the Holy Spirit, and Philip, and Prochorus, and Nicanor, and Timon, and Parmenas, and Nicolaus, a proselyte of Antioch.

think our current church model causes a lot of spiritual gifts to lie dormant. Without continual opportunities to exercise our spiritual gifts, many believers don't even discover them. Not to mention, we already established how Christ demonstrates his power through us in a unique way as long as we have complete unity. But how can we have complete unity when only a small portion of the priesthood of all believers gets to fully operate in their callings?

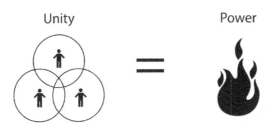

Of course, we can rationalize the discrepancy between the signs and wonders we read about in the early church versus today's churches by telling ourselves we simply have a "different expression" of church today. But that is like saying a clipped and caged bird is merely a "different expression" of a bird. The same God that created birds to fly created his people with spiritual gifts. Sadly, we often bury our spiritual gifts like the frightened servant who buried his master's gold rather than investing it like he was commanded.[2]

But this is actually exciting news. If God's intentions for his church remain unchanged and he still lavishes spiritual gifts upon his people, then he is probably ready to do some pretty amazing things whenever he finds a group of people who are ready to reclaim their calling as a priesthood of all believers.

---

2   **Matthew 25:25** So I was afraid, and I went and hid your talent in the ground. Here you have what is yours.

The Priesthood of All Believers

Earlier we saw how the Israelites refused to go up the mountain to meet with God; instead they asked Moses to go for them and bring back the Lord's instructions. We also saw how they rejected God's kingship and asked for a mortal king to rule over them instead. And throughout this book, I have tried to make the case that the institutional church model installs a pastor as the proxy for the priesthood of all believers.

If all this is true, clearly God's people follow a distinct pattern. And that pattern seems to point to a problem. Apparently, we desperately want someone else to take responsibility for our relationship with God.[1] And simply divesting ourselves of church buildings, programs, positions and titles may not get to the root of this problem. So, what should we do about it? Well, there is at least one thing we probably should not do.

Once we find a few other believers who are willing to pursue genuine church community with us, we probably shouldn't be in too much of a hurry to appoint leaders. The first order of business should be reclaiming our calling as a priesthood of all believers and relearning how to function as the Body of Christ. In other words, we may need to submit ourselves to the sole Headship of Christ for awhile before we even consider recognizing elders in the church.

---

1   **Judges 9:8-15** One day the trees went out to anoint a king for themselves. They said to the olive tree, "Be our king." But the olive tree answered, "Should I give up my oil, by which both gods and humans are honored, to hold sway over the trees?" Next, the trees said to the fig tree, "Come and be our king." But the fig tree replied, "Should I give up my fruit, so good and sweet, to hold sway over the trees?" Then the trees said to the vine, "Come and be our king." But the vine answered, "Should I give up my wine, which cheers both gods and humans, to hold sway over the trees?" Finally all the trees said to the thornbush, "Come and be our king ... "

This is especially true in American church culture, where we tend to have an unnatural fixation with leadership.

Such statements are probably shocking to some readers. If you have spent much time in the institutional church, you may have been exposed to the unbiblical idea that every church member needs some kind of human spiritual authority, such as a pastor, to serve as their "spiritual covering." Without a spiritual covering, we are told a believer is somehow spiritually unprotected and clearly outside of God's will.

There are a couple of problems with this idea. First, there is the practical question: if believers cannot stand on their own without a superior as their spiritual covering, who is the pastor's spiritual covering? After all, he is the pinnacle of the spiritual pyramid. (Or if he is part of a larger pyramid, such as a denomination, we can simply apply the same question to the person or persons at the top of that pyramid instead.)

The "Spiritual Covering" Myth

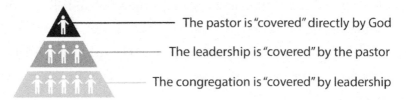

—— The pastor is "covered" directly by God

— The leadership is "covered" by the pastor

—— The congregation is "covered" by leadership

There is usually one of two possible answers to this question: either the pastor is directly covered by Christ; or else he submits himself to a group of peers such as his fellow pastors. But that just raises another question: if the pastor can stand alone before God or simply submit himself to a small group of equals, why can't we?

If God and a few friends are sufficient for the pastor, why are they not sufficient for us?

Secondly, there is the more serious issue: there are no scriptures that support the idea of a human spiritual covering in the New Testament church. As we saw earlier, Christ is our sole mediator. To suggest he cannot fulfill this role on his own contradicts a multitude of scriptures, including Romans 14:4:

> Who are you to pass judgment on the servant of another? It is before his own master that he stands or falls. And he will be upheld, for the Lord is able to make him stand.

Also, how do we explain the fact that the church in Antioch functioned without elders, possibly for years? This means they were a church without any leadership other than Christ for quite some time.

In Acts 11:21, we see the believers in Antioch come to the faith. We are told in Acts 11:26 that Barnabas and Paul (then called Saul) met with the church for a whole year. Afterward, from Acts 13:4 to Acts 14:21, we see Paul and Barnabas traveling to numerous cities, including Iconium where they "remained for a long time"[2] before eventually returning to Antioch. Finally, in Acts 14:23, they appointed elders in the church.

So, what exactly did the believers in Antioch do during the time between the church being formed and elders being appointed? Since there are 58 "one another[s]" in the New Testament, it is very likely they were simply learning how to function as a priesthood of all

---

2   **Acts 14:3** So they remained for a long time, speaking boldly for the Lord, who bore witness to the word of his grace, granting signs and wonders to be done by their hands.

believers. As we noted earlier, members of the early church were expected to instruct one another, correct one another, minister to one another through psalms, hymns and spiritual songs, confess their sins to one another, pray for one another, heal one another, etc.

Or consider Hebrews 12:14, 15. In this passage, like so many others, all the believers in the church are instructed to look out for one another:

> Follow peace with all men, and holiness, without which no man shall see the Lord: Looking diligently lest any man fail of the grace of God ... (KJV).

However, our English translations cause us to miss the full significance of this verse. The Greek word we translate as "looking diligently" is actually *episkopeō* which means to oversee. It is derived from the same root as *episkopos*, which we translate as "overseer", whom we now know is the church elder. Therefore, this passage is actually informing us it is the job of all church members to oversee one another, not just the elders.

So, maybe we have it all backward. Rather than being in a big hurry to appoint spiritual leaders in the hopes of producing some kind of amazing church culture, maybe it actually takes an amazing church culture to produce genuine spiritual leaders. Perhaps it takes a spiritual furnace to forge an authentic elder in the first place.

If so, then we do not need to rush the process. Producing leaders is Christ's responsibility; he can raise up elders whenever he thinks the timing is right. In the meantime, we simply need to focus on Christ.

Christ Alone

If you read the introduction to this book, you know my very first memories of Christian community were rooted in the Jesus Movement and living in a Christian commune. On the other end of the spectrum, I eventually became an institutional church pastor. I preached sermons, officiated weddings, spoke at funerals, ran programs, recruited volunteers, coordinated events, organized mission trips, as well as many other clerical duties. In order to speak with authority about the two forms of church discussed in this book, I clearly needed to experience both. And I needed to experience them as someone who was fully invested, not as an outside observer. Thankfully, I can honestly say I experienced God in all of it.

However, I eventually concluded the church was never meant to become a corporation. It is an extension of the community of God, both the Body of Christ and his Bride. But just as Adam and Eve were offered a choice between the tree of knowledge and the tree of life, when it comes to living in spiritual community, every church must choose whether to focus on rules and regulations or relationships. That includes non-institutional churches as well. Just as Adam and Eve were deceived into trying to apprehend something they already had, we must be on our guard not to let our longing for genuine church community become the thing that ruins us for genuine church community.

If we get too wrapped up in what is and isn't church, we will take our eyes off Christ and end up making rules and regulations about how to do and be the church. A church that makes its focus the way we do church will eventually cease to be a genuine church community. That is because a genuine church community is solely focused on Christ.

<table>
<tr><td align="center">Rules</td><td align="center">Relationships</td></tr>
</table>

A loving husband or wife cannot become an exceptional spouse by constantly looking inward, becoming fixated on whether or not they are a good spouse. That would be deceptively self-centered. A truly great husband or wife simply abandons all thoughts of self, looks outward, and loves his or her partner.

And so it is with the Bride of Christ. The church is solely Christ's concern; Christ is the church's sole concern. Even if our rules are nothing but rules against making rules, we can still end up trying to exert our own ideas about the church over others or use them as an excuse to withdraw from others. Either way, we will be left with our own pet ecclesiology but no real church community. We must never take our eyes off Christ, even in an effort to please him. Much like Jesus's counter-intuitive command to "seek first the kingdom",[1] the way to unlock our calling as a genuine church community is to remain focused on Christ, not by becoming distracted by all our ideas about genuine church community.

Then why even write a book like this? If all our ideas about how to do church must eventually end up on the altar, then why bother

---

1   **Matthew 6:33** But seek first the kingdom of God and his righteousness, and all these things will be added to you.

writing a book about how we do church? Because the one idea this generation needs to abandon is today's church corporation. Jesus laid down his life for a Bride, not to launch an organization. We need to reawaken to that reality; we need a fresh revelation of what it means to be the Bride of Christ, to re-learn how to be small Christian communities that operate like extended spiritual families. We need to reclaim our calling as a priesthood of all believers and reinstate Christ as the sole Head of our congregations.

Since we are reaching the end of our time together, I thought it only fitting to share what is surely the most famous description of the early church. It takes place immediately after the birth of the church on the Day of Pentecost, after the disciples had gathered in complete unity and been baptized in the Holy Spirit.

The only caveat I would like to add before sharing this passage regards the phrase, "attending the temple together and breaking bread in their homes." Many of today's churches try to use this line as a sort of proof text that the first believers had "big church" and "small groups": big church meetings in the temple and smaller church meetings in their homes. However, this is simply not true.

The very first Christians (the ones described in this particular passage) were Jews who received the revelation that Christ was their long awaited Messiah. They didn't think of Christianity as a new religion but as the fulfillment of all the Old Covenant promises. In fact, the term *Christian* didn't even come about until the Gospel spread to the Gentiles.[2]

This means the believers described in this passage considered themselves Jews who simply had the revelation about Jesus. Therefore, it makes perfect sense they continued to go to the temple. Besides the fact they could now experience Christ in all the powerful

---

2   **Acts 11:26** And in Antioch the disciples were first called Christians.

symbolism of the Old Covenant worship, this was also the perfect place to spread the Good News about Jesus to their fellow Jews.

However, once the Gospel spread to the Gentiles, they did not require Gentile believers to adopt Jewish practices such as meeting in an Old Testament style temple. We saw that quite clearly in our discussion about Acts 15. There is absolutely no basis to believe the temple gatherings mentioned in this passage are analogous to today's organized church gatherings.

Anyway, now that we have been on this journey together, my hope is that you can read this passage without filtering it through an institutional church lens. I pray you can glimpse whatever picture the Lord wants to reveal to you, to stir whatever longings he has placed inside you regarding his church. Now, let's look at the amazing church community described in Acts 2:41–47:

> So those who received his word were baptized, and there were added that day about three thousand souls. And they devoted themselves to the apostles' teaching and the fellowship, to the breaking of bread and the prayers. And awe came upon every soul, and many wonders and signs were being done through the apostles. And all who believed were together and had all things in common. And they were selling their possessions and belongings and distributing the proceeds to all, as any had need. And day by day, attending the temple together and breaking bread in their homes, they received their food with glad and generous hearts, praising God and having favor with all the people. And the Lord added to their number day by day those who were being saved.

Does that sound like the type of church community you have been looking for? Is it very different from the original ideas you had about church when you first started reading this book? Or has this whole discussion felt like using smoke and mirrors to paint an overly romanticized portrait of the early church while looking for loopholes to discredit today's church model?

In My Defense

Throughout this book, I have cited various scriptures. At times, I have used widely accepted interpretations of certain verses; at other times, I have suggested somewhat radical interpretations of other verses. For example, take Mark 10:42, 43, the passage where Jesus warned his disciples not to be like the Gentiles. I asked you to entertain the idea that Jesus might have been warning his disciples against adding hierarchy, positions and titles to the church. I even went so far as to suggest he could have been speaking prophetically since this is exactly what the Gentiles would do one day.

Even though I have tried to introduce such ideas as possibilities rather than assertions, I expect such an approach has left some readers with more than a few unanswered questions. For instance, can I settle the matter of what Jesus actually meant in these verses? Can I prove one way or the other whether he was talking about institutionalizing the church? And if not, then why even introduce such a possibility? Couldn't I build a stronger case with a more straightforward argument? Wouldn't it be better to stick to points which are more easily provable?

Honestly, the answer is "no." I cannot prove some of the more radical possibilities I have proposed. And truth be told, it was never my intention to do so. Then why use them to build my case about church? The answer is simple: because I am not trying to build a case. Quite the contrary, I am only trying to cast doubts on the case that already exists, the case for institutionalizing the church. You see, if this were a courtroom trial, I would be the *defense*, not the *prosecution*. In such a scenario, it would be the job of the prosecution to build a case for institutionalizing the church.

The prosecution is the one responsible for shouldering the burden of proof. In this case, the prosecution would be the one who has to build an argument "beyond any reasonable shadow of a doubt" that it is perfectly scriptural to deviate so far from the biblical example of the early church. The job of the defense, on the other hand, is to simply cast doubts on the prosecution's case, to create that "shadow of a doubt."

Was Jesus literally warning us against institutionalizing the church in Mark 10? Who can say for sure? But even the slightest possibility should make us less cavalier about turning a genuine church community into a corporation. We should prayerfully seek the Holy Spirit and find out whether or not we are despising our birthright and handing over our identity to a corporation, simply for the sake of tax breaks and limited liability.

But wait. Why exactly do I think I am the defense and not the prosecution? Isn't this whole book just one big attack on the institutional church? By no means! It is merely a defense against it. It is an attempt to preserve genuine church community.

The picture of church I have painted (or at least tried to paint) in this book is the one plainly portrayed in Scripture. Therefore, it is the starting point for any discussion about the way we do church. Just as the defendant is innocent until proven guilty, the biblical example of the early church should serve as our pattern unless there is a clear case from Scripture that proves otherwise.

Though there are many things we do not know about the early church, the picture I have attempted to paint is based on the things we do know, things that are not open to debate, non-negotiables. For instance, we know the early church was comprised of small communities of believers who met in ordinary homes. We know Christ was present in a powerful way, performing wonders in their midst. We know the church took care of the poor. We know they had spiritual fathers and mothers. We know certain members specialized in equipping other members for ministry. And we know every believer was expected to participate as a fellow priest.

Yet somehow, we have become so indoctrinated with our institutional church perspective that we unconsciously re-interpret the descriptions of the early church every time we read them. What do I mean? Well, let's look at a common example. How do most of today's churchgoers read Ephesians 4:11? Do they take this verse at face value or filter it through an institutional church lens? Here is what it says:

> So Christ himself gave the apostles, the prophets, the evangelists, the pastors and teachers ... (NIV).

As we discussed earlier, this is the one and only time the word *pastor* is used in the Bible. There is no description of a pastor's duties and no mention of a pastor being in charge of the church. He is simply listed second-to-last in a succession of persons such as apostles and prophets. Nonetheless, whenever we happen upon this single use of the word "pastor," we impose our existing ideas onto it.

We imagine a person who is responsible for leading a church, for preaching weekly sermons, for officiating weddings, and speaking at funerals, and christening babies, and baptizing new believers. But where does this picture come from? Certainly not from Scripture! Clearly, it comes from traditions that were added over time as the church became more and more institutionalized. This doesn't mean we shouldn't have traditions. But our understanding of the Bible should be the basis of our traditions, not the other way around.

Now that you have read this book, I hope you will consider prayerfully re-reading the New Testament with fresh eyes, without filtering the text through the lens of man-made tradition. And I pray you rediscover God's original intentions for his church and become inspired to seek out genuine church community with other believers. And I hope you find a church that functions like an extended spiritual family, the kind of community you were created for.

The Church Exodus

This book was primarily written for believers who are on either side of the transition from attending an institutional church to joining a genuine church community. But let me be clear: this book wasn't written to try to convince anyone to leave the institutional church; it was simply written to validate and empower those who already have a growing conviction to do so. I cannot make the assumption God is specifically calling you to leave the institutional church; that is between you and the Lord. However, it certainly seems like he is calling plenty of others.

According to a recent survey,[1] the number of non-churchgoers in America has grown by 38 million over the past 10 years, which is an increase of more than 30%. To put this in perspective, that is more people than the entire population of Australia (24 million) or the entire population of Canada (36 million).

Australia	Non-churchgoers	Canada

24 million	38 million	36 million

And keep in mind, we are only talking about the people who recently joined the ranks of non-churchgoers. The total number of non-churchgoers has grown to 156 million. In fact, if all the

---

1   http://www.onenewsnow.com/church/2014/12/15/10-things-you-didn-t-
     know-about-unchurched-americans

non-churchgoers in America became their own separate nation, it would be the eighth most populated country on the planet.

Also, the younger a person is, the less likely they are to attend church. It seems each new generation is less interested in church than the generation before. Yet even though people seem increasingly disinterested in church, they are not disinterested in Jesus. In fact, the majority of non-churchgoers in America still consider themselves Christians. And most of these non-churchgoing Christians say they are "actively seeking" something better than what they have spiritually experienced so far.

Depending on your point of view, these statistics are either bad news or good news. If you think the church is an organization, then this is bad news because our membership is declining fast. However, if you think the organized church model is something that needs to be discarded, then this is good news; the church finally seems to be emerging from her institutional internment. Obviously, one perspective is more optimistic than the other.

But what about those believers who want to leave but somehow can't find the nerve? Some believers are simply afraid of what might happen if they quit going to church. I'm not just talking about the loss of friends or reputation but the spiritual consequences. They are afraid of stepping out from under the "spiritual covering" of their pastor, of falling prey to the enemy, maybe even losing their faith. Since we already addressed the spiritual covering superstition, we will not revisit it here.

Perhaps more churchgoers might jump at the chance to leave if they already had a place to land. If there were an existing non-institutional church community nearby, a lot of churchgoers might work up the courage to jump ship. But heading out into the great unknown seems to be asking a lot. So, here are a couple of thoughts that might help:

We are called to walk by faith, not by sight.[2] The matter of whether or not to leave the institutional church is not about being able to see around the corner and know what's coming before making a decision; it is simply about obeying whatever God tells you to do. If you are uncertain, by all means, wait for confirmation. It is a big decision; don't take it lightly. But if everyone waited for someone else to go first, no one would ever do anything. And let's face it, if you made it this far in the book, there is a strong possibility God might be calling you to leave, even if you don't have a clear destination yet.

Although you might have heard a couple of sermons that make you feel guilty whenever you think about not going to church, the problem exists in the very premise; the church isn't something you go to; it's something you are. Paul tells us plainly that the parts of the Body never cease being parts of the Body.[3] Therefore, you will continue to be part of the church whether or not you ever set foot in an institutional church building again.

Also, why be scared to lose something you don't really have? These organizations we call "churches" are not actually churches anyway. That doesn't mean the people inside are not part of the church universal. But a church corporation is not a genuine church community. So, why are you afraid to stop "going to church" when you haven't been part of an actual church yet? If you leave the institutional church and don't find genuine church community right away, you haven't "quit going to church." You have simply gone

---

2   2 Corinthians 5:7 For we walk by faith, not by sight.

3   1 Corinthians 12:15, 16 Now if the foot should say, "Because I am not a hand, I do not belong to the body," it would not for that reason stop being part of the body. And if the ear should say, "Because I am not an eye, I do not belong to the body," it would not for that reason stop being part of the body.

from one non-church-experience to another. And at least you have taken a real step toward finding genuine church community.

That's not to say there aren't risks for some people to leave the institutional church. If all your Bible study, prayer, fellowship, service, and worship have depended upon organized church services, programs, and events, you will need to take ownership of your own spiritual life. You will have to become intentional about getting together with other believers, praying, studying, worshiping, and so on. But in many ways, this can be very liberating. Like going from infancy to adulthood, you can move from spiritual dependence to independence.

And that is probably the best reason not to rush the process. Much like you would not want an eighteen-year-old to rush from living with mom and dad straight into marriage, it is usually a bad idea for believers to go straight from the institutional church into genuine church community. Just as a young man might need to move out on his own, find his footing, discover his identity, and get some sense of direction before he is ready to become a good husband, you probably need to explore your own spiritual independence for awhile after you leave the institutional church.

Of course, independence does not mean isolation. If you cut yourself off from other believers, you will be making a dangerous mistake, much like putting a tourniquet on a perfectly healthy limb. You need fellowship with other believers. That is why Hebrews 10:24, 25 tells us:

> And let us consider how to stir up one another to love
> and good works, not neglecting to meet together, as
> is the habit of some, but encouraging one another …

Even though being absent from Sunday morning services doesn't cut you off from the Body, there are plenty of legitimate ways to cut yourself off from the Body. This will not only cause immediate problems; it will also undermine the ultimate goal behind finding your spiritual independence in the first place. Eventually, you need to graduate to something greater than independence, and that is interdependence. And true spiritual interdependence can only be found in genuine church community.

Just like we see in the relationships within the Godhead, in the way Adam and Eve related to each other before the Fall, in the many descriptions of mutual submission within the early church, the whole reason to find your independence is so you can willingly lay down your life in service to God and others. If you skip over the season where you find your spiritual independence, if you try to go straight from dependence to interdependence, you will enter into genuine church community with a lot of expectations that can never be met. It is not unlike entering a marriage, expecting the other person to make you happy rather than having a heartfelt desire to serve your spouse.

I am sometimes concerned whenever I hear people in non-institutional church circles use the term "detox" to describe the time between leaving the institutional church and finding genuine church community. This time is also described as "wandering in the desert." And both of those descriptions are very true. (In fact, I have used those same descriptions myself.) But they are also incomplete.

Yes, God has led a lot of us through a season of desert detox to purge some bad habits and ideas we picked up in the institutional church system. But if detox is all this time is about, then it is simply a bad season we must endure; it's a painful process we will be in a hurry to get through, much like a spiritual root canal. However, we do not want to be like that young man who is in such a hurry to get married that he rushes through one of the most defining times of his life.

Instead, I would encourage you to embrace the season between your exit from the institutional church and your eventual entry into genuine church community. It is truly exciting to discover your spiritual independence, to learn that God alone is sufficient. Take some time to detox and unlearn, to "unchurch," if you will. And do not waste time nursing old hurts or desperately searching for your new tribe. In time, God will take care of both. Instead, focus on deepening your relationship with him and sharing the overflow of that relationship with others.

Your Own Exodus

If this book has emboldened you to leave the organized church or if it found its way to you shortly after you left, I would like to encourage you. I know from experience how difficult that transition can be. Frankly, you might be in for some awkward conversations.

Have you figured out how to explain your decision to family, friends, and church leaders? Have you thought about what to say whenever you bump into former church members who ask questions like, "Where do you go to church now?" If not, I would like to share a few thoughts that might help.

There is an amazing little scene at the end of the Gospel of John where Jesus calls Peter to follow him again. Peter then notices John trailing behind them and asks, "Lord, what about him?" Christ's answer is profound. In John 21:22, he essentially says (and I'm paraphrasing here), "What business is that of yours what I want of him? You must follow me, no matter what."

Once you know for a fact God has called you to do something, all other concerns are non-issues. That's the very first thing you must settle within yourself. Even if you can't explain your decision to others, that doesn't change what God has called you to do.

This is not to say there isn't a right way to go about leaving the institutional church. However, the need to make others fully understand can often be self-serving. If God has called you to leave the organized church, what does that have to do with what others think about it? And if he wants them to remain in the institutional church until he returns, what is that to you? With that being said, here are some considerations that might help you navigate these waters:

Out of respect for your church leaders, you may want to inform them of your decision to leave. But if they do not agree with your decision, your only recourse is to agree to disagree. The important thing is to give them the respect of speaking with them, rather than just disappearing from Sunday morning services. You may never get your pastor's approval; trying to press for it may actually be harmful. After all, how would that work out? If you sat down with your church leaders and reasoned through the scriptures together until you finally came to the same conclusions about church, you may satisfy your need for approval but where does that leave your leaders? Assuming they are genuinely called to the institutional church, wouldn't this revelation only discourage them in their calling?

Similarly, you do not need fellow church members to approve or even understand your decision. Therefore, you do not need to go around broadcasting everything God is revealing to you about the church. That doesn't mean you cannot test the waters to see if he is calling others in your circle to go on this journey with you. But if you find yourself debating or recruiting, you're only sewing division in the church. This probably means you are worrying too much about your own reputation, that you are overly-concerned about being misunderstood. You need to be prepared to follow Christ, even if others think you are a heretic.

Along those lines, you do not need to go out in a blaze of glory. There's no need to make any sort of announcement or send a churchwide email or post a detailed explanation on your Facebook page or family blog. (Yes, I have a blog that talks quite boldly about the institutional church, but I didn't start blogging in earnest until about 10 years after I resigned as a pastor.) If possible, you need to leave the institutional church gracefully, without burning any bridges. After all, others might need to cross those same bridges later.

After you leave the organized church, then what? Although there isn't a single prescription that works for everyone, please consider taking some time to detox and find your spiritual independence, as we already discussed. As long as you are prayerfully seeking genuine church community, whenever the timing is right, God can connect you with others who are on a similar journey.

In the meantime, I hope you will connect with me through my Unchurching blog (www.unchurching.com). My hope is to get enough people to sign up for my mailing list that it reaches a tipping point. Eventually, I would like to see unchurching.com become an online tool for connecting unchurching believers in the real world. Other sites have attempted to do something similar but they never reached a critical mass where real-world connections were very practical. So, if this is something that interests you, please help spread the word about this book and the blog.

On the site, you will find several animated videos, cartoons, and information about my new podcast which builds upon many of the ideas I've shared in this book. If you have a work commute, I highly recommend downloading a few episodes and checking them out on your way to work.

Also, if you have already found others who are willing to join you on your journey, and your group is ready to take the next step, I would love to suggest some other resources that might help. Please feel free to email me at **richard@unchurching.com**. I look forward to hearing from you.

Made in the USA
Las Vegas, NV
05 November 2024

11140776R00125